Tales of O

Other counties in this series include:

Avon
Bedfordshire
Berkshire
Buckinghamshire
Cambridgeshire
Derbyshire
Devon
East Anglia
Essex
Gloucestershire
Hampshire
Herefordshire
Hertfordshire
Kent
Leicestershire

Lincolnshire
Norfolk
Northamptonshire
Nottinghamshire
Oxfordshire
Shropshire
Somerset
Staffordshire
Suffolk
Surrey
Sussex
Warwickshire
West Yorkshire
Wiltshire
Worcestershire

Tales of
Old Cornwall

~

Sheila Bird

With illustrations by Don Osmond

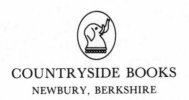

COUNTRYSIDE BOOKS
NEWBURY, BERKSHIRE

First Published 1992
© Sheila Bird 1992

COUNTRYSIDE BOOKS
3 CATHERINE ROAD
NEWBURY, BERKSHIRE

ISBN 1 85306 212 X

Cover Design by Mon Mohan
Produced through MRM Associates Ltd., Reading
Typeset by Paragon Typesetters, Queensferry
Printed in England by J W Arrowsmith Ltd., Bristol

To my eldest niece, Catherine

Contents

CONTENTS

CORNWALL – The map overleaf is by John Speede, and shows the county as it was in the early seventeenth century.

CONTENTS

CORNWALL – The map overleaf is by John Speede, and shows the county as it was in the early seventeenth century.

An Octogenarian's Epic Walk

THE statuesque, handsome fishwives of Newlyn in their scarlet cloaks, long navy skirts, crisp white aprons, smart buckled shoes and comely broad brimmed black hats were much admired for their classical style and easy grace, a fact which they took advantage of. No wonder artists found inspiration in Newlyn's colourful, work-a-day scene. Newlyn has long been a thriving fishing port and it was customary for the fishermen's wives, who had a strong line of cheerful patter, to hawk their husband's catches through the streets, tunefully crying their wares. They transported incredibly heavy loads of fish in specially shaped baskets or cowals, which were supported on their backs, with broad bands passing across their foreheads and through their headgear. It was the balancing of such weights which gave rise to their poise and upright bearing.

One such was Mary Kelynack, born on Christmas Day 1766, married into a well known fishing and seafaring family and with a fondness for colourful exploits and gaining media attention. She may not have been the girl she once was, her dark, flirtatious eyes and sensual charms now dimmed, but old Mary still had the gift of the gab and an engaging personality which she used to good effect. Well aware of the possible effect of the fishwives' fresh and rustic charms in the dusty, dreary metropolis, she hit on the singular notion of walking to London, purportedly to attend the Great Exhibition of 1851.

11

But in doing so she had hopes of generating some publicity which might hold sway with the authorities in regard to a Naval pension which she seemed to believe she may be entitled to.

Despite all the fuss and concern, or more probably on account of it, this game and enterprising octogenarian went ahead with the plan, revelling in all the attention and the prospect of enjoying more of the limelight when she reached the big city. Old Mary set forth in a blaze of publicity, looking every inch the part in her fishwife's apparel and carrying a cowal suspended from her head and shoulders, endearing herself to all who saw her. She had declared from the start that she would accept no help along the way, apart from money, so the hundreds who turned out to cheer her and wish her well were generous in contributing to her funds. The old lady was well able to handle the publicity, and had a flair for accepting their financial help and goodwill gracefully, with what she felt was an apt word or two. An example of this occurred when she reached Camborne, and a well known grocer named Shackerley presented her with a half sovereign and wished her God's speed for the journey. She thanked him kindly, then added as an afterthought, 'Three cheers for Chatham', meaning William Pitt, Earl of Chatham, whose family had connections with Boconnoc, which was miles away from Camborne.

The fishwives of Newlyn had to be strong and healthy to survive their everyday workload, but it is incredible that the old lady actually walked the 300 or so miles to the capital, when going by coach or horse was reckoned to be a test of endurance. For as the old rhyme said:

'Ride to Lunnon on a hoss? See what money it do cost.
Rub us raw and rub us beer, afore we do get 'aalf way theer!'

Mary must have had remarkable feet. But she accomplished her walk, for on October 25th 1851, *The Illustrated London News* reported: 'On Tuesday, among the visitors to the Mansion House was Mary Kelynack, 84 years of age, who had travelled on foot from Penzance, carrying a basket on her head, with the object of visiting the Exhibition and of paying her respects

12

personally to the Lord Mayor and Lady Mayoress.' When the ordinary business was over, Mary was escorted to the justice room, where the Lord Mayor said, 'Well, I understand Mrs Kelynack you have come to see me.' 'Yes,' replied our Mary, 'God bless you.' And looking round a trifle overawed, added, 'I never was in such a place before as this.'

People were warming to the pert old lady with spirit and charm, and soft Cornish accent; and she knew it. As a 'character', she could get away with saying things that other people could not, and she decided to strike while the iron was hot. 'I have come up asking for a small sum of money,' she said, and added, 'I am eighty four.' This remark may have been a reference to her plea to the Admiralty; or it may not, and if the Mayor felt slightly taken aback, he did not show it. 'Where do you come from?' he inquired, politely. 'From the Land's End,' replied Mary. Surely everyone knew the Land's End; it had been a famous landmark for centuries. Or was it her broad, Cornish dialect that he did not quite understand? 'Er...From what part?' he asked. 'Penzance,' replied Mary.

Unabashed by the elevated company and grand surroundings, she went on to tell the Lord Mayor and the assembled company about her long walk to London, which had taken five weeks. His Worship, puzzled about the need for such a test of endurance, ventured to ask, 'What induced you to come to London?' Mary explained that she had a little business to attend to, and also thought it would be a good opportunity to see the exhibition. 'I was there yesterday, and I mean to go again tomorrow,' she declared. On being asked what she thought of it, she replied that she thought it was very good.

She stood admiring the resplendent surroundings, then casually let drop that she had precisely 5½d to her name. With Mary, it was not so much what she said, but the disarming way in which she said it, and after some light-hearted but seemly chat, the Lord Mayor presented her with a sovereign, and urged her to take good care of it as there were a lot of thieves in London. Our heroine, touched by such unexpected generosity suddenly burst into tears, saying, 'Now I will be able to get back home!' Unaccustomed as they were to floods of feminine tears in the manly environment of the Mansion House, she was whisked away to the housekeeper's room to have a nice cup of tea with the Mayoress. 'There's nothing like a good cup of tea, is there?' said the Mayoress, kindly. 'No. I prefer a 'andsome cuppa tea to all the best wines in the Kingdom!' confessed our forthright fishwife. Then she made her departure, thanking them for all their kindness.

For Mary, now staying in Marylebone, this was a prelude to other heady experiences still to be savoured, for she had her portrait painted, gave sittings for the Cornish sculptor Nevill Northey Burnard, was an honoured guest at Greenwich Hospital and other prestigious places, and to crown it all, was presented to Queen Victoria and Prince Albert on her final visit to the exhibition. Mary, who had captured the imagination of the sophisticated capital, also made an impression on Queen Victoria, who recorded in her diary: 'The old Cornish woman, who walked up several hundred miles to see the Exhibition was at the door to see me – a most hale, old woman, who was near crying at my looking at her.'

The Illustrated London News, which had taken to Mary in a big way, concluded, albeit a trifle condescendingly:

'She possesses her faculties unimpaired; is very cheerful, has a considerable amount of humour in her composition; and is withal a woman of strong common sense, and frequently makes remarks that are very shrewd, when her great age and defective education are taken into account. She is fully aware that she has made herself somewhat famous; and among other things which she contemplates, is on her return to Cornwall, to end her days in Paul Parish, where she wishes to be interred by the side of old Dolly Pentreath, who was also a native of Paul.'

It could be added that Dolly Pentreath also employed a wide repertoire of colourful antics which found her a place in history, by virtue of her claim to be the last speaker of the Cornish language.

If *The Illustrated London News* saw Mary as a lovable innocent abroad, *The West Briton* saw her as a knowing opportunist, and reported in November:

'This Cornish octogenarian, who walked to London to see the Crystal Palace, and was so kindly received by the Lord Mayor and Lady Mayoress, has returned home after an absence of two months, with her pockets well lined through the benevolence of the Londoners. We understand that on the route homewards she received much kindness. Mr Prockter, of Launceston, sent a letter to the aged woman whilst she was in the metropolis, inviting her, on her return, to take a seat inside the 'Times' coach from Exeter to Truro, free of charge, of which favourable opportunity she availed herself on Thursday week. She was also hospitably entertained on her journey by Messrs Pratt, of Exeter, Prockter, of Launceston, and Lenderyou, of Truro, at whose hotel she slept on Thursday night. Her appearance at Launceston excited considerable curiosity, and the Mayor, with a number of ladies and gentlemen visited her at the White Hart Hotel, where they presented her with money and useful gifts.'

Mary, pleased no doubt to be home after all the excitement, entertained local folk with her tales of the high life in the big city, until her death, four years later.

Three
Wise Men

S UPERSTITION was rife throughout the Cornish countryside
in the 19th century, when illness, strange happenings or
calamity were attributed to the devil and his hags, either as
direct retribution from the spirit world, or as the result of ill-
wishing by a black witch, who was usually some innocent
neighbour, unfortunate enough to be old and ugly. Black
witches were responsible for the spread of evil, and white
witches, in the guise of charmers, pellars, conjurors, wise men
or wizards, were the only ones gifted enough to free ordinary
mortals from their spells – at a price! Cautious folk, believing
that prevention was better than cure, made secret, annual visits
to the local witch or wise man as a sort of insurance policy for
the next year. Most towns and villages had their own
practitioner, and if the truth were known, few of the population,
rich or poor could genuinely claim to be untouched by all this.
Although people openly made fun of the naivety of others, one
could never be too sure; better safe than sorry!

Consultations were held in the homes of the practitioners,
who also made periodic perambulations around the countryside.
Although many of them were rogues, they inspired hope and
confidence, brought about many cures and were even helpful
in maintaining law and order. For if money went missing or
some other crime were committed, the threat of the wise man
being brought in, was enough to make the culprit confess, and

attempt to restore the status quo. In effect, they were precursors of our present day social services rolled into one, with a strong emphasis on care in the community.

Magical powers were deemed to have passed from fathers to daughters and from mothers to sons, although being the son of a seventh son, or born a 'footling' (entering the world feet first), helped. However, most of the characters who adopted this dubious way of life were self-styled. Artfulness, quick-thinking and the ability to avoid a tight situation were essential qualifications for any aspiring wizard, as three such, Johnny the Hooper, the Pellar of Nanstallan and the Wise Man of Illogan, amply demonstrated.

Johnny Hooper blazed a trail around these parts in the early part of the last century, and what he lacked in skill, he made up for in unswerving self-confidence, for he persuaded the gullible that his success was due to scholarly learning and clean living. To re-inforce this notion, he placed lighted candles in the fields around his cottage, to create an image of sweetness and light. His speciality was the charming of ill-wished cattle.

The Pellar of Nanstallan featured in *The West Briton* in 1856:

'It is humiliating to think that there are such characters as gipsies, witches, conjurors, fortune tellers, and charmers living now, in this nineteenth century, and artfully earning a livelihood out of the credulity of mankind. And, strange to tell, vast numbers of people love to have it so. If they are out of health, or lose animals by disease or accident, they straightway conclude that they are bewitched, and away they go to the professed conjuror. It used to be Johnny Hooper, of Ladock; it is now Mr – Thomas, of Nanstallan, in the parish of Bodmin. This man carries on a flourishing trade in the conjuring way, and seldom goes home from a fair or market quite sober, and withall is an immoderate snuff taker.' However, the said gentleman was to receive his cum-uppance on the way home from market, when he was waylaid, beaten up and robbed by one of his victims. So he took the hint, moved further to the west and resumed his wily way of life.

Perhaps the best known of the 19th century colourful Cornish conjurors was the self-styled wizard, Dr Jimmy Thomas, also known as the Wise Man of Illogan. This flamboyant character, tall and stooping, 'all legs and wings', and quite a showman, was frequently seen around the Roseland, with his horse and cart and carpet bag brimming over with spell books and other tricks of the trade. His strange appearance was heightened by being almost bald on one side, for he employed the bizarre ritual of plucking hairs from the right side of his head and casting them over his left shoulder. After performing various feats and capers with long drawn out incantations and mumbo jumbo, calculated to frighten and impress, he would feign fatigue, hoping that people would find additional coins for his efforts. He was married to Tammy Blee (Tamsin Blight), the famous white witch of Helston, who was generally well liked and far more successful than he.

The Wise Man of Illogan also held surgeries at his home, which were regularly attended by tinners and sea captains, in the hope that things would augur well for them in their dangerous occupations. There was a certain unease in the waiting room, because of the shame of being seen there; but they were all in the same boat. On one occasion, a patient, rather more sceptical than most, got tired of waiting, and expressed his impatience by suggesting that the old boy ought to employ an assistant. Shocked fellow patients told him it would be more fitting to employ the waiting time in humble prayer.

The great man, like others of his breed, had instilled in his clients fear and obedience; anything which happened between them and their physician must never be revealed. For betraying that trust would not only invalidate the healing; it would result in dire consequences. Dr Thomas had more reason than most to fear exposure. He had a penchant for prescribing spells in bed requiring his overnight attendance, and as time went by it would seem that some of his male patients were becoming multi-ill-wished; a situation which the physician would have them believe, required more and more of his attention. When the scandal broke, Tammy left him and he performed one of his well-rehearsed disappearing tricks. But he returned to Cornwall two years later.

Some might have discerned a certain element of poetic justice in his final cum-uppance, which came after he had taken advantage of a sick man seeking his help. *The Royal Cornwall Gazette* reported in 1874:

'James Thomas, of Broadlane, Illogan, known as 'Dr Jimmy Thomas, the Wizard', died suddenly at his house on Wednesday morning. It appears that a man named John Odgers, of Camborne, who is unwell, believing himself to be ill-wished, consulted Thomas, who told him in order to get the spell removed it would be necessary for him to sleep with him (Thomas). He, therefore, did so. Odgers having risen shortly before eight on Wednesday morning, Thomas requested him to light the fire and get the tea ready for breakfast whilst he (Thomas) dressed himself. Odgers had not been in the kitchen long before he heard a noise in the chamber. On going upstairs, he found Thomas on the floor insensible, and soon afterwards he was a corpse... Death has taken away a rather remarkable member of society, 'Dr' Thomas, holding just the same position among a certain class of society as the medicine man of the North American Indians and other savage tribes, is among the fast disappearing race of witches and wizards. Still they have their representatives, perhaps, in the nineteenth century in the 'mediums' of the Spiritualists.'

Interestingly, the Zennor poet 'Henna' Quick had felt much the same way a century earlier, when he wrote:

'The Cornish drolls are dead, each one;
The fairies from their haunts have gone;
There's scarce a witch in all the land,
The world has grown so learn'd and grand.'

Salty Old Town

FALMOUTH has one of the finest natural harbours in the world, and the famous haven, with its steeply wooded shores and wealth of navigable creeks capable of accommodating hundreds of vessels in time of storm was well known to early mariners. Over the centuries ships from every nation have called here, and the sound of foreign tongues and a miscellany of nautical noises echoed round the quaysides. Ships and craft of every kind once graced the handsome harbour, which was always busy with arrivals and departures and humming with news from near and far. For the rollicking, rumbustious life of Falmouth town revolved around the needs of ships and sailors, and the blessings and curses, triumphs and tragedies brought in by the sea. Jolly jack tars, pirates and merchants, smugglers and wreckers, worthies and villains, cut throats and heroes have thronged these narrow streets and alleyways. Dubious ladies festooned secluded doorways, members of the dreaded press gang lurked and pounced, and sounds of ribald laughter, singing, shouting and brawling rang out upon the evening air from the numerous taverns in the town.

The quaysides were busy scenes of excitement, noise, bustle and all the trappings of travel and maritime commerce. Amidst all the fuss, bemused disembarking passengers tended to subscribe to the philosophical theory that ports were the habitat of birds of prey or birds of passage; the one preying on the

20

other. Having braved the hazards of sea travel, they would stay overnight in an adjacent hostelry, trying to blot out those industrious sounds and get a wink of sleep before being subjected to the spine-jerking trials of overland travel on the bumpy roads of those days.

There was a time when the ships of the King's Navy sailed from Falmouth, and in the palmy days of the Post Office Packet Service the riches of the world were landed on these quaysides. 'Falmouth for orders', which had a stylish ring about it, was a phrase known everywhere. Falmouth has had its fluctuating fates and fortunes, but few ports could ever have played such a far-ranging variety of salty roles than this port with its 'last out, first in' situation. Falmouth had the advantage of being the last port of call for vessels leaving the English Channel, who might want provisions and servicing before facing the perils of the Atlantic. By the same token, returning vessels which had taken a battering at sea, or needed re-victualling after long voyages would call here for repair and shelter, and their crews could take advantage of the many facilities that existed for seafarers here. So Falmouth was the 'last out' or 'first in' port, before or after encountering an awful lot of sea.

As well as being a port of refuge and centre of ship construction and ship repair, Falmouth has been a packet station, mercantile port, ocean terminal, base for ocean-going tugs, site of a lifeboat station and an important pilchard fishery; all of which gave rise to the ship-to-shore trade and a host of maritime services and institutions. Not only that, Falmouth has also played an important role in times of threatened enemy invasion. The port had been a temporary naval base in time of war, carrying out ship chandlery and victualling for the Admiralty, and was a point of troop and convoy assembly in more recent times. Troops landed here after the evacuation of Dunkirk, while D-Day landing craft, constructed locally in great secrecy, put to sea off Falmouth. The heroic attack on the German U-boat port of St Nazaire, code named Operation Chariot was launched from here.

21

In view of all this heady success and glamour it seems surprising that the potential of Falmouth was not recognised earlier, for initially it was the poor relation of Penryn, that ancient port and cultural centre, and Truro, which, like Penryn, was neatly tucked out of sight and safe from piratical visitations, and had the advantage of being on convenient overland routes. But the security of Falmouth was improved in the time of Henry VIII, with the emplacement of the twin fortifications of Pendennis and St Mawes at the mouth of the harbour, following skirmishes with the Spanish and French along the coast and up the river.

The town of Falmouth began to take shape in Elizabethan times. It was Sir Walter Raleigh, homeward bound from the coast of Guinea who saw the potential of the Fal estuary as a deep water anchorage of some importance, when only one dwelling and the mansion of Arwenack occupied these shores. When he reached London he made representations to the Queen's Council for the establishment of a port and settlement, able to offer facilities and carry out services for ships and their crews. It was the piratical, wealthy and powerful family of Killigrew who dwelt in Arwenack which put these ideas into practice, much to the dismay of Penryn, Truro and Helston, destined to lose much of their trade to Falmouth. Within a comparatively short time the quayside developed into a settlement of some consequence, with its own market. Sir Peter Killigrew had the Custom House removed from Penryn to this new town, which did not please the inhabitants of Penryn, while generations of Truronian mayors struggled to retain their ancient rights over Falmouth port and harbour, which they eventually lost in a court battle.

In 1660 a royal proclamation declared that this place, formerly named Smithicke and Pen-y-cum-cuic should henceforth be known as Falmouth. A year later Falmouth received its charter, having demonstrated its Royalist loyalties in the time of the Civil War, by withstanding a six month siege at Pendennis Castle. These were prestigious days indeed, but

Falmouth's Golden Age was yet to come.

From its advantageous situation near the entrance to the English Channel and the Western Approaches, Falmouth speedily became the first port of Cornwall, and was chosen in 1688 as the site for the highly prestigious Post Office Packet Station. This was an exciting, brutal age of enterprise and endeavour, with scope for swashbuckling exploits on the grand scale, demanding valour and endurance. Initially the run was to Corunna and Lisbon, but this was extended down to the West Indies and parts of North America. Observers of the day commented on Falmouth being full of rich merchants, growing wealthier with the undercover commerce opened up by the packet trade with Portugal. For at Lisbon the King's ships were claiming the privilege of being immune from the attentions of nosy customs officers, and were carrying large quantities of British merchandise which they sold on board to eager Portuguese traders, who got the goods ashore without paying any duty. When the Portuguese authorities got wind of this they complained to the English government, which agreed that it was unfair to honest traders. But this lucrative sideline of the packet seafarers continued, albeit more furtively, and the merchants artfully devised a scheme whereby Portuguese vessels carried gold in the form of bars or moidores (coins), for dealing with sophisticated London traders.

Not surprisingly, the packet ships carrying these valuable cargoes attracted the attentions of other ruthless characters, including the dreaded Algerian pirates, Spanish and American privateers and French men o'war. So the brave seamen manning these packet ships had an extraordinary range of hazards to contend with in the course of their day-to-day lives. But as carriers of mail, albeit armed, they were under orders not to fight unless attacked, and if cornered, to sink the mails and surrender. Throughout the 18th century the packet ships were recognised conveyors of worldwide news, with responsibility for private and commercial mail and naval and military dispatches. Look outs on the shore scanned the horizon

23

for signs of approaching sails, and at a given sign a flotilla of fast gigs would race out to try to secure the all-important ship-to-shore trade. The lightest and most important mail would be dispatched speedily to the capital by mail coach, while heavier packages were loaded onto local haulier Russell's waggons to make their lumbering way to London. Transporting such wealth added highwaymen and robbers to the other formidable hazards of road travel at that time, and armed guards were employed to accompany such mail.

During the 18th and 19th centuries, naval vessels carried out reconnaissance operations and protected convoys. The Admiralty created a dockyard at Mylor Churchtown to supply water and victuals to their vessels, then later armaments and equipment, and naval vessels came to be repaired there instead of at Plymouth. The Admiralty took over the operation of the packet service in 1832, because of the wartime situation, replacing the packet ships with small sloops of war. But sadly, many of these armed brigs, deep waisted and low decked, were in poor shape, and many lives were lost on account of their unseaworthiness. Their pre-disposition to disappear without trace, along with their unfortunate passengers, cargoes and mails, earned them the grim nickname of 'coffin brigs.' These vessels could be seen leaving and entering the harbour under clouds of canvas yet only too often they were sighted struggling home across the bay with battered hull, shattered masts and spars, torn sails and dismantled guns, having survived a bloody skirmish at sea.

It was a tremendous blow for Falmouth when the prestigious Post Office Packet Service was finally transferred to Southampton in 1852. The proud era of Falmouth's packet ships began to decline as sail gave way to steam, and Southampton, more centrally situated for the rest of Britain, with good rail links and the facilities to accommodate the new steamships was seen as more viable as a seat of maritime commerce than salty old Falmouth, with its remote situation and old fashioned, horse-drawn transport. Fortunately for Falmouth, fishing was still going well, and a group of visionaries had seen the potential for an important dockyard to be sited here, exploiting that 'last out, first in' advantage.

Shoppers and sightseers passing the memorial situated on The Moor, to those gallant men of the glorious days of the Falmouth Packets, might well pause for reflection in these less adventurous days.

The
Diabolical Provost

CHRISTIANITY came early to Cornwall, and religious foundations were established on well appointed sites. Settlements, still known as 'churchtowns', grew up around these churches, and for centuries the word of God was preached in the old Cornish language.

The effects of the Reformation, particularly the forbidding of the use of the Roman Catholic Mass, were unpopular, and the pressures to conform with the New English Prayer Book were particularly resented by the Cornish, who, for the most part, did not understand the language. Throughout Cornwall there were rebellions against the Protestant reforms. The murder of a royal commissioner committed inside Helston church by a priest from St Keverne in 1548 gives some indication of the passions which had been aroused, and which resulted in the loss of many lives. The Provost Marshall Sir Anthony Kingston was set the task of bringing the Cornish rebels to justice, and on entering the county sent a polite letter to the Mayor of Bodmin to say he would be passing through and would welcome the opportunity of being entertained to dinner. The Mayor, much flattered, went to a great deal of trouble to ensure that his hospitality would be fitting for such exalted company and the Provost and his followers were given a warm and courteous welcome which they would never forget.

Everyone was on their best behaviour and things were going

well, but just before they went in to dine, Kingston took his host on one side confiding in his ear that one of the townsfolk was to be executed, and requesting that the gallows might be erected and ready for use by the time the feast was over. The Mayor discreetly made arrangements for this to be done, and everyone sat down to a hearty meal in congenial company.

When the meal was over, Sir Anthony turned to the Mayor and asked whether the little arrangement had been completed on time. On being assured that everything had been made ready, he took his host's arm in courtly style, demanding with an air of grandeur, 'Prithee, lead me to the place.' Then, beholding the grim gallows with the eye of a connoisseur, enquired as to whether the gallows were strong enough. The Mayor confirmed that they were. 'Well, then,' ordered his dinner guest, 'Get thee up there speedily, for thou hast prepared thine own execution!' Disbelieving, hoping he was the victim of a joke yet trembling with fear, the Mayor demanded that Sir Anthony admit that it was all just a terrifying hoax. 'In faith!' roared the Provost. 'Dost thou not comprehend?... there be no remedy. For thou hath been a busy rebel, and doth pay the price!' Then without further ceremony the Mayor of Bodmin was strung up and speedily dispatched before the eyes of the whole assembly.

Hearing the news of recent events, an artful local miller, who had been active in the uprising, feared a visitation by the Provost and decided to make a timely departure from home, instructing his faithful assistant to stand in for him. 'If anyone do come a-calling, thou art to say, "I be the Master. I be the miller millin' 'ere the last three year".' Sure enough the callous Provost did appear, and requested to see the miller. 'I be the Master 'ere,' declared the miller's lad, swelling with importance. The visitor looked him up and down contemptuously. 'So thou art the Master, eh? If that be so, how long hath thou been a miller here?' 'I bin millin' 'ere three year!' declared the simple soul, thereby sealing his fate. 'Lay hold on him!' commanded the Provost. 'For, verily this be the man we seek. String the

28

villain up and hang him from yonder tree!' 'I be no villain! I be no Master! I be only the miller's man!' cried the frightened lad as he was manhandled by the officers of the justice, 'Truly I be!' 'A likely story!' sneered the officers. 'The simpleton doth change his story to seek to save his neck!'

'Nay, nay, good friend,' sneered the Provost, with mock sincerity. 'I taketh thee at thy word; truly I do. If thou beest the miller, thou knowest thou art a rebel. And if thou beest merely the miller's man, as thou now sayeth, then thou art nothing but a lying knave. And howsoever, thou canst never do thy master better service than to hang for him!' And without further ado the lad was strung from the tree, and made to pay the price for his master's misdeeds.

In the face of this kind of retribution, the rebellious Cornishmen were eventually brought to obey the King's will.

Her Face
was
Her Fortune

WEEK St Mary, situated on wild and windy terrain where
ridge roads converged, found a place in history as the
romantic setting of a true rags-to-riches story, which began
around 1450 with the birth of a little girl to a humble farming
family.

Eking out a meagre livelihood was never easy around these
parts, where generations of hardy folk had coaxed and cultivated
the barren soil, enriched it with manure and reared their flocks
and herds on the exposed pasturelands. Traditionally whole
families engaged in the taxing business of farming the land in
this time-honoured style.

Thus it was one fine and fateful morning, that a pretty young
shepherdess called Thomasine was tending her sheep and flock
of geese up on Greenamore, when Richard Bunsby, a wealthy
London merchant, came riding by. Catching sight of the fair
maiden in the meadow, he suddenly came to a halt, turned the
horse around and called to ask her if she would be kind enough
to tell him the way. Did he really pay much attention to what
she was saying, or was he preoccupied with her fresh-faced rustic
beauty, natural grace and charm? As a married man, romance,
of course, was out of the question. But would not such a comely

servant be a tremendous asset in his important household? Surely such a pretty creature should not be out there working in the rude and windswept fields? Nature must have created her for something more than this.

After engaging her in conversation for quite some time, the stranger begged leave to speak with her parents. And he put it to them that their daughter was exceptional and was cut out for greater things. If he might be allowed to take her to London, she could become a servant in his fine household, well paid, protected and privileged; they need never want for anything for the rest of their days. Whether it was his bulging saddlebags, flattering attentions and overwhelming importance, or promises of a better life for their beloved daughter that inspired their confidence and trust we shall never know; but depart with him she did. She must have been a brave, adventurous girl to be parted from her family and all that was familiar to her, in favour of an unknown destiny in the faraway metropolis.

Things went well for the humble farmer's daughter from Cornwall, who fitted in well with the staff of the city draper's household, mixing easily above stairs in every type of company, and impressing everybody with her pleasing looks, good heartedness and gentle manners. Some time after the death of the lady of the house, who had been so kind to her, she humbly accepted a proposal of marriage and made a fitting wife for her employer, who provided amply for her on his demise a few months later.

The well-mannered, elegant young widow, who had by now added wealth and culture to her considerable assets, had many admirers, and became much sought after in the higher echelons of society. Many young and not-so-young hopefuls came a-courting, but she rejected them all in favour of Mr Gall, a wealthy member of the Worshipful Company of Merchant Adventurers. After a few more years of nuptial bliss and increasing recognition, she once again found herself widowed and the beneficiary of a second fortune, thereby becoming one of the wealthiest and most desirable ladies in London. So when the former Cornish shepherdess ventured into the matrimonial state for the third time, the groom John Percival, who had aspirations to rise within the Corporation of the City of London, found himself the envy of many. How proud John Percival and his wife must have felt in 1499, when, his ambitions achieved, he was elected Lord Mayor of London and knighted by the King. Sir John and Dame Thomasine Percival enjoyed some happy years together, but it was to be demonstrated yet again that the constitution of a Londoner was no match for a wilding of the moors, and she found herself a widow for the third time.

Having savoured the fashionable life of the metropolis, and achieved a hat-trick in husbands and fortunes, our heroine demonstrated a yearning for her roots and the simple pleasures of life by returning to Week St Mary, where she spent the remainder of her days in charitable pursuits. In these Thomasine's three husbands and family were not forgotten, for she founded a chantry where she might pray for their souls,and a grammar school where the sons of the gentlemen of Devon and Cornwall were educated. Other good works included the repairing of churches, the construction of roads and bridges, the endowing of almshouses for unmarried ladies and the provision of food and clothing for the poor.

Thus the local community remained indebted to the lady who began life as a humble shepherdess, and gained the name of Thomasine Bonaventure in retrospect.

Parson Dodge
to the Rescue!

O VER two centuries ago, humble folk lived in fear and
dread of the spirit world, and sought some means of
protection from such ills. Recognising that need in Cornwall,
there was no shortage of parsons keen to demonstrate their
influence over these spirits; a situation which fed superstition
and helped the men of the cloth gain a tighter control over their
innocent flocks.

Life was particularly hard for the rural folk in Cornwall, who
had traditionally enjoyed the rights of common land to help
them eke out a frugal existence by growing their own vegetables,
keeping a few animals and hunting wild game for the pot. But
human nature being what it is, certain greedy landowners
sought to enclose the common land and claim it as their own
without due regard for anyone else. Indeed, in the 17th century
two wealthy landowners were in bitter dispute with each other
about the acquisition of the common near Lanreath, in East
Cornwall. The matter was taken to court, and the situation was
so fraught with animosity that the loser flew into a violent rage
and died. Few mourned his passing, but many were to fear his
antics from beyond the grave.

When it comes to being preoccupied with the material things
of this life, the philosophical might subscribe to the theory that
'you can't take it with you'. But this ambitious loser apparently
reckoned that he would have a good try, or at least ensure that

no one else would enjoy it. The artful old devil returned to haunt the common! He appeared as a black apparition driving a phantom carriage across the moors, drawn by a team of headless horses and generally creating pandemonium. Local folk going home across the moors took to their heels in terror. The news spread like wildfire, gaining additional, dramatic details in the telling, until the entire population reached a state of panic. 'We'll go to the vicar', they said. 'He's a man of the cloth who understands these things. He'll know what to do'. So they went to the vicar.

The mild-mannered vicar of Lanreath listened to their stories, which seemed to get more and more outrageous, and did his best to re-assure them, but they demanded action. And so it was that the sexton of Lanreath found himself on his way to Parson Dodge at his vicarage in the village of Talland, bearing a note from the vicar of Lanreath, requesting help in resolving a disturbing situation which was terrifying his parishioners. He had heard about Parson Dodge, who was celebrated in dealing with such problems; everybody had heard about the old parson and his colourful exploits with fiendish spirits, for his fame had spread far and wide.

The old, grey vicarage with its heavy chimneys, graceful gables and mellow, mullioned windows lurked in those days behind high walls, trees and shrubs, providing an apt setting for one with such a reputation. The sexton nervously tied up his trusty horse, opened the squeaky gate and lifted the big brass knocker on the hefty oak door. A young servant girl tripped along to open it, and asked him to come inside. Whereupon he was shown along dark, dank passages and into the sunless parlour where the great man sat, looking scholarly and thoughtful. As the reverend gentleman looked at the letter he was clearly startled, but as he read and re-read the letter, he assumed an air of coolness and mastery. 'Er . . . Yes. Are the villagers really as frightened as this letter would imply?' he inquired, in matter-of-fact tones. 'If you please, Sir, they be truly terrified. Folks doesn't sleep well in their beds o' nights

35

for fear of the evil spirit. An' every night it do seem to git nearer. 'Fore long 'twill be in the village, an' then wot shall us do?' The vicar questioned the sexton closely as to the nature of the strange phenomenon. 'I ain't seen one o' those, but I see'd the ghost an' 'is 'eadless 'orses an' the carriage wot rides across the sky o' nights . . . . Well, not acherly *see'd*. But we 'eard 'un! Me an' my good lady, we 'eard 'un! We 'eard all the c'mmotion an' the racin' wheels. "Ghostly coach wheels, they be", I says to me good wife, an' she be that afear'd. Please, yer Reverence, you be the one us do need. Everyone do know as 'ow spirits be terrified o' Parson Dodge. Please 'elp we.' If the modest parson felt his ego being inflated, he did his best not to show it. 'Pray, tell your vicar that I'm busy tomorrow, but will come over to Lanreath the following evening', he declared evenly, before turning his attentions to other matters.

Two nights later Parson Dodge and the Vicar of Lanreath set off for the moor on horseback to investigate the haunting. If the moor looked somewhat bleak and inhospitable on a winter's day, it looked decidedly more so on a winter's night, as eerie winds whistled around the trees and isolated homesteads, and swept across the open wasteland, carrying with it the dismal sounds of dogs baying in the distance. Although uneasy, each adopted a certain air of bravado, to impress the other, and to convince themselves of their unswerving trust in the Divine. They bravely patrolled the bleak and lonely landscape and looked for sinister signs, but nothing seemed to be brewing.

With mixed relief and disappointment, they decided to abandon the attempt. 'It was good of you to have come', said the parson of Lanreath. 'We'll try again some other time', replied his ghost-laying colleague. 'We'll choose a night that's more conducive to spirits; the sort of night that draws them to their former haunts.' So saying, they each departed their separate ways, for the vicar of Lanreath made straight for his rectory, while Mr Dodge tried a short cut back to Talland.

Parson Dodge's old grey mare ambled amiably along the

track until they reached the valley bottom near Blackadon, when she began to show signs of distress. She started whinneying, then came to a halt and refused to go any further. When her master attempted to urge her forwards, she moved backwards, and when he dug in his spurs and lashed with his whip, she became more frightened, pranced about and threw up her haunches. He dismounted and tried to lead her gently forward by the reins, but she would not have it. He re-mounted and tried to proceed, but she refused to move forward. When he dropped the reins, she backed, turned around and re-traced their route.

In shades of darkness the profile of the moor seemed to be altering. The mare became distressed as changing, indefinable shapes became more menacing, until they took on the form of the fearful, black spectre with his coach and headless horses. Then Parson Dodge beheld the ghostly driver, whip in hand standing over a cowering figure on the ground, which could only be his fellow parson. With cool head and iron nerve, our celebrated layer-of-ghosts summoned up a prayer, but before he could give it utterance, the fearful spectre became aware of a superior presence and exclaimed, 'Dodge is come! I must be gone!' (Or at least, that is what the good man reported later.) Whereupon he leapt into his chariot and disappeared beyond the dark horizon.

In the meantime the other horse had taken flight and bolted, and the folk of Lanreath were awakened by the clattering sound of horse's hooves. Some panicked, thinking this was the arrival of the phantom come to haunt them; others recognised it as the vicar's horse, and realised that something was amiss. So they set off for the moor, where they found their vicar senseless in the arms of Parson Dodge. The victim's eyelids began to flicker, but he was in such a state of shock that he had to be carried home by his parishioners. Happily the adventure ended here, for the incoherent clergyman soon recovered from his ordeal and returned to the pulpit to preach the Good Word to his flock. And as for the phantom mischief-maker, neither he, his headless horses nor his chariot were ever seen again.

A Case of
Early Industrial
Espionage

TODAY, walkers on the cliffs at Poldhu, to the north of Mullion, will find an imposing granite monument on the windswept summit, where Marconi's Wireless Telegraphy Station once stood. And therein hangs a tale of enterprise, rivalry and early industrial espionage.

Guglielmo Marconi, who was born in Bologna on 25th April 1874, of Italian and Irish parentage, was privately educated in Italy, at Bologna, Florence and Leghorn. Throughout his schooldays he had displayed an aptitude for physical and electrical science, and a preoccupation with the theory that electrical waves could be used to convey telegraphy signals. His work brought him the Nobel Prize for Physics in 1909, recognising his role in opening up this field of communication which was to benefit mankind.

In 1896, young Guglielmo came to England hoping to obtain a British patent for his apparatus, and as luck would have it, he met Sir William Preece, the Chief Engineer of the British Post Office, who recognised his talent and gave him the opportunity to carry out further research in this country. They looked around for a suitable site to establish a research station, and chose Poldhu on the Lizard peninsula for its advantageous geographical situation. Marconi's Wireless Telegraphy Company took root in 1900, and it was from here on 12th December 1901 that the first wireless signal was transmitted across the Atlantic to Newfoundland. It was an exciting new development with far reaching implications for the future.

This area had long established its lead in communications by land and sea, initially with visual signalling. In early times watchers on the shore had given warning of enemy invasion by sending up flares to initiate the lighting of beacon fires around the coast, with messages relayed by semaphore from headland to headland. Opposite Marconi's research station, on the other side of Mount's Bay, was situated the Eastern Telegraph Company. Set up at Porthcurno in the 1870s, the company enjoyed the prestige of being known as 'the home of cable telegraphy'. Responsible for the laying of ocean cables and on-going developments in radio communications, they had monopolised the world communications field for some time. Now, with the installation of Marconi's station, this toe of Cornwall became the eye, the ear and the tongue of the nation's intelligence operations. Secrets of war and peace, life and death, success and failure, love and hate and every conceivable type of news, monumental or trivial has vibrated across the landscape, through the air and beneath these Cornish waters.

The Marconi complex, with its spidery towers, dominated a wild and windswept headland on a beautiful section of the Cornish coast. It was closely guarded, and always shrouded in secrecy. Those who were employed there were not allowed to divulge any information about the place, and were quick to hasten inquisitive lingerers on their way, directing them to the lane skirting the complex. No wonder it was regarded with suspicion by local folk and as an environmental eyesore by the tourists of the day. From a distance Marconi's paraphernalia resembled four Eiffel Towers, encircled by white staircases leading to fragile platforms, set amid a sea of white masts, like a vast marina, with a maze of wiring suspended overhead. To walk this headland which Marconi had annexed was to step out in company with arcades of these overhead wires, stretched from pole to pole at regular intervals. A walker, bemused by the scene, stopped to ask an old man working in a cabbage patch what he made of it all. The gardener straightened his back, looked thoughtful for a few moments and said, 'I be too old i' the tooth to be bothered about they new fangled things. I do giv 'un the go-by! Yer, I do giv 'un the go-by', then returned his attentions to cultivating cabbages.

Those at the heart of the Marconi endeavours would have been happier, no doubt, had other people subscribed to that philosophy. One section of the community which did not, was situated about 20 miles across Mount's Bay at Porthcurno. The Eastern Telegraph company was determined to discover just what was going on at this upstart, rival establishment beneath their very noses, which was attracting world-wide acclaim. Why all the secrecy? They intended to find out and they would have to be underhand about it.

Today's walkers at Pedn an mere, known locally as Wireless Point, half a mile to the west of Porthcurno, may notice a curious structure incorporating large iron hoops at the highest point, resembling a tool of medieval deterrence. It is the hinged base of a giant wooden mast which played an important role in the dawning history of industrial espionage, for this was the Eastern Telegraph company's secret weapon. They had hit on the notion of setting up a secret listening station to allow them to eavesdrop on what was going on. The wooden mast, made up of three sections of pitchpine, was fashioned by Messrs. N. Holman & Sons of Penzance. Getting the abnormally long and heavy load through the intervening narrow, winding lanes with a team of horses was a further test of ingenuity. It required the removal of some hedges and inch by inch manoeuvring. Having been successfully transported to the cliff edge, the towering mast, 170 ft high when assembled, had to be carefully hoisted into position with the aid of powerful jacks and a complicated system of pulley blocks and sheer brute force.

The exact nature of the experiments carried out at Poldhu

may never be known, for they were likely to have been highly sensitive, and whatever records those eavesdroppers may have kept have not survived to the present day at Porthcurno.

During the First World War the advantages of communication without the laying and maintaining of cables was recognised, but the other side of the coin was that important messages could be overheard by others. So information, disinformation and artfully coded communiqués became part of the wartime strategy, and wireless communication was used at the battlefront. The unwieldy early sets, difficult to transport over rough terrain, caught the attention of the enemy and became the targets of machine gun fire; a situation which hastened the development of more sophisticated, compact equipment for use in the field. Progress in the use of wireless in aeroplanes was similarly hastened. The Royal Navy had been making use of Marconi's equipment since the turn of the century, and as time went by enemy interception, direction finding (locating bearings of transmitting stations) espionage and counter-espionage was being carried out from proliferating stations across seas and continents. The Marconi Company and the GPO operated a number of direction finding stations around our coasts, which were more favourably situated than those of the Germans, and therefore more accurate in obtaining data. Thus the invention of wireless opened up whole new dimensions in war and peace, and drastically changed the age old art of warfare.

The rapid developments in technology changed the emphasis in communications worldwide, with workers fearing for their jobs in times of recession, and the policy was towards re-organisation and amalgamation. In local folklore, mystery surrounds the sudden closure of Marconi's station at Poldhu, and rumours still circulate as to what actually went on there. But eventually the Eastern Telegraph Company at Porthcurno became a combined network of radio and cable stations known as Cable & Wireless. Another walker at Poldhu in 1935 placed on record that the wireless masts which used to rule the whole

Lizard landscape with an austere and purposeful dignity had gone for ever. However, records at Porthcurno state that part of the site remained in intermittent use until the outbreak of the Second World War, when the equipment was impounded for 'security reasons'.

Today's walker on the Lizard might regard these relics as a fascinating insight into industrial archaeology, and gaze in wonder at the well poised, giant dishes at Goonhilly, reaching for the skies.

The
Valiant Lifeboatmen
of Padstow

'From Padstow Point to Lundy Light
Is a sailors' grave by day and night.'

CORNWALL'S wild and inhospitable Atlantic coast, offering little protection from the raging storm, was notorious among seafarers in the days of sail, and by a sad irony the refuges that did exist presented hazards of entry. The haven of Padstow, with its glorious golden sands much beloved by artists and holidaymakers, has a dangerous sandbar just inside its protective headlands which has been the graveyard of numberless ships and their ill-fated crews. Some say that this curse of mariners was placed there by a petulant mermaid, in retaliation for a rascally son of Padstow firing his crossbow at her as she playfully frolicked in the surf. Be that as it may, the offending sandbar has resisted repeated attempts at clearance and continues to collect its victims.

Padstow was well to the fore in taking measures to prevent shipwreck, and to offer humanitarian help to the victims of shipwreck in the setting up of the Padstow Harbour Association. This progressive organisation was formed in 1829 'for the purpose of saving life and property from shipwreck by rendering assistance to vessels entering the port in distress'. Supported

by voluntary means, no salvage claims were made other than recovering out-of-pocket expenses, which were promptly ploughed back into the enterprise. Their highly ambitious undertakings included pilotage, the operation of lifeboats, the emplacement of navigational aids, dealing with all aspects of the aftermath of shipwreck and major engineering feats such as the cutting back of Stepper Point. This helped to reduce the disastrous effects of baffling winds, which drove brave little sailing vessels attempting to make for a safe haven helplessly onto the Doom Bar. The daymark on Stepper Point and the handsome old pilots' cottages at Hawker's Cove are reminders of this remarkably enterprising organisation, motivated by humanitarian needs, which over the course of time became aligned with and eventually taken over by the Royal National Lifeboat Institution. Doom Bar and the restriction of the tides created on-going problems for the operation of Padstow's lifeboats, which were placed at Hawker's Cove and afloat in the harbour until the establishment of today's fine lifeboat station on Trevose Head, offering fast launch by slipway directly into Mother Ivey's Bay.

The Padstow lifeboat has always been manned by particularly fine and courageous men of the sea, as befits this maritime county. The story of Padstow's lifeboats is a gallant and inspirational one, reaching the heights of heroism and the depths of tragedy, when those who sought to save the lives of strangers in distress at sea, paid the ultimate price for their devotion to duty. Daniel Shea, who was coxswain from 1855 to 1862 and continued to serve as a volunteer after that, was a thoroughgoing seafarer of the Old School. He emerges today, alongside Henry Tregidgo and Matt Lethbridge, as one of the three most decorated lifeboatmen in Cornwall. He had three Silver Medals to his credit and other honours for gallantry in the course of saving life from shipwreck. His service at Padstow was typical of the terrible challenges which these brave Cornish lifeboatmen chose to face.

Shipwrecks occurred around these shores with appalling

regularity in the days of sail, but the gales of March and October threw up a formidable crop of casualties over the centuries. March 1859 certainly kept the Padstow lifeboat crew on their mettle. On the eighth day of that month the Padstow lifeboat *Albert Edward,* rowed by six oars, launched to the aid of the French brigantine *Gonsalve* of Nantes, which after being embayed off Padstow, had managed to get free, only to be caught by eddying winds at the entrance to the harbour and driven relentlessly onto the dreaded Doom Bar, leaving her crew in dire peril. The courageous lifeboatmen fought their way through the angry waves, which repeatedly broke over the little lifeboat, and managed to rescue seven crewmen and land them safely on the shore.

A week later, when the lifeboatmen were just beginning to relish the drama in comfortable retrospect over their pints in the town's little taverns, the schooner *Frederick William* of Ipswich was caught out in just the same way during a fierce north-westerly gale. Again the lifeboatmen launched into terrific seas, taking off four crewmen and a pilot, and conveyed them to the safety of the shore. With due regard to these two services and general exemplary conduct, Coxswain Daniel Shea, Commissioned Boatman of the Coastguard received the Silver Medal of the Institution, and his crew the customary monetary awards. The French Emperor also recognised the service to the *Gonsalve* by the presentation of Silver Medals to each member of the crew.

The following year found the men of the Padstow boat assisting with others to land the crew of the ship *James Alexander* of Liverpool, which was wrecked off Padstow during a very heavy gale on 22nd January. Further recognition went to Coxswain Daniel Shea, who was now Chief Boatman of the Coastguard, adding a second service clasp to his Silver Medal for his role in the rescue. 'Thanks of the Institution' went to lifeboat hero William H. Tregidgo, formerly of the Bude lifeboat, and now Chief Officer of the Coastguard at Newquay for their services.

December 29th, 1865 saw Padstow's most famous service, to the barque *Juliet* of Greenock, which also became the glorious twelfth mission to a vessel in distress for the heroic Daniel Shea, now a volunteer lifeboatman in Padstow's third lifeboat, *Albert Edward II.* At a time when ferocious west-south-westerly winds, combined with a flowing tide and heavy ground sea were proving Hell Bay to be aptly named, the *Juliet,* which had been bound from Demerara to London with a cargo of rum and sugar, was rolling heavily and flying her ensign at half mast to signify her distress.

Christmas excesses were forgotten when the signal was spotted, and cries rang out through the narrow streets, 'Shipwreck on Doom Bar! Shipwreck on Doom Bar! Man the Lifeboat!' And the brave sons of Padstow dropped what they were doing, took to their heels and speedily launched the lifeboat into the most daunting of conditions. The wind was in their tail on the outward trip, accelerating their progress, but presenting the danger of being flung end over end. Having got within a cable's length (608 ft) of the *Juliet,* they anchored and allowed the lifeboat to drift towards the stricken vessel. Then, daringly anticipating the rise and fall of the waves, they took up a vulnerable position under her stern, to give the trapped crewmen the opportunity to jump down into the lifeboat one by one as directed. Time was running out as they snatched the captain to safety, and manoeuvred the lifeboat back to her anchor.

If things had been difficult thus far they were now faced with the even more demanding task of battling with sail and oar against the cruel elements, with the added weight of 17 shivering sailors. The seas were running high, but by now the state of the tide was such that negotiating the narrow, deep water channel back to Hawker's Cove brought them dead to windward. It was a near-impossible task, and Coxswain William Hills had the responsibility of deciding whether to go outside the harbour with the tide and weather and proceed up the coast to Port Isaac, or continue this dangerous and exhaustive battle with the elements. The strength and stamina of these early lifeboat crews is almost beyond belief. For these tough men of the sea who had little or no food to sustain them and were exposed to the vagaries of the weather, knew that they were ultimately dependent on their own muscle power if they were to survive. With sheer determination they managed to reach Hawker's Cove, assisted in the exhaustive pulling and skilful manoeuvring by the sailors they had saved. The barque was pounded to pieces by nightfall and most of her cargo had been flung up on the Polzeath shores. By a strange irony, the only person to lose his life in that fearful episode was one William Ham, who was so excited about the prospect of collecting free rum from the shipwreck that he rushed down to the beach and drank himself to death.

The Master of the *Juliet* said afterwards: 'Had the lifeboat not come to our assistance, all hands must surely have perished, and I cannot speak in terms too strong to express my sense of the conduct of the boat's crew in risking their lives in such a gale'. For this heroic service, Coxswain William Hills was awarded the Silver Medal of the RNLI, while ex-Coxswain Daniel Shea who had been a crewman on this occasion received a third service clasp to his Silver Medal. Memorials inside Padstow church and the windswept cemetery at the top of the hill remind us of lifeboatmen who paid the ultimate price for their devotion to duty in the grand humanitarian cause of preserving life from shipwreck. The simple marble tablet inside the church completes the story of Daniel Shea's heroic career. For it states:

In memory of
Daniel Shea, Chief Officer of Coastguards, 2nd Class
William Intross, Chief Boatman
Thomas Varco, Commissioned Boatman
Andrew Truscott, Trinity Pilot
Michael Crennel, Mariner
'These brave men perished on the Albert Edward lifeboat,
while nobly endeavouring to assist the crew of the Georgiana,
of Boston, Lincs., at the entrance to Padstow harbour, on the
6th February, 1867.'

'The Lord hath his way in the whirlwind and the storm.'
Nahum 1 3.
'The will of the Lord be done.' Acts 21 14

Daniel Shea's service to the aid of the schooner *Georgiana* of
Boston, Lincolnshire, yet another victim of the dreaded Doom Bar,
was to be his 13th. The lifeboat *Albert Edward II* launched into
mountainous seas, with a strong following wind, and as was
standard practice in such conditions, the lifeboat was streaming
her drogue (sea anchor) aft, to gain stability and lessen the chances
of capsizing. Then disaster struck. The drogue rope, weighted down
by an enormous volume of water suddenly snapped, releasing
terrific pent-up energy which caused the lifeboat to catapult almost
end over end flinging most of her crew into the boiling surf.
Capsized for a second time which left her upside down, she then
righted herself and was driven ashore on the sands, none the worse
for her experiences. Some of the horrified spectators on the cliffs
rushed down to help. Eight crewmen were saved, but five were
lost. Could anything be more moving than when brave men
staunchly set out in the face of danger to save the lives of strangers
only to lose their own?

The gallant Daniel Shea had answered the summons to every
distress call during his time on station, and had helped in saving
55 lives from shipwreck. For him the contemporary verse by
'Dagonet' came all too true:
'Been out in the life boat often?
Aye, aye, Sir, often enough.
When it's rougher than this?
Why, bless you, this ain't what we calls rough!
It's when there's a gale a-blowing
And the white seas roll in and break
On the shore with a roar like thunder,
And the tall cliffs seem to shake,
And the sea is a hell of waters,
And the bravest holds his breath,
As he hears the cry for the lifeboat
His summons may be to his death.'

49

The
Eccentric Edgcumbes

BORDERING the western shores of Plymouth Sound lies the well appointed estate of Mount Edgcumbe. The estate came into the possession of the Edgcumbe family by marriage and a genuine purpose built artificial ruin was constructed on the green sward in 1741 to impress their rivals. But then, the ancient family of Edgcumbes was not unaccustomed to the quaint and bizarre. In 1742, one of the Edgcumbes, mother of the first baronet Sir Richard, suffered a very strange experience – and lived to tell the tale!

It seems that the poor lady had been taken ill and lapsed into a coma, to be subsequently presumed dead. She was given a decent burial in the family vault beneath the chapel at Cotehele and left there to rest in eternal peace. This would have been the end of the matter had it not been for a ghoulish and dishonest sexton who, on the night after the funeral, had the audacity to creep down to the vault, force open the coffin and divest the lifeless fingers of their priceless rings. Perhaps the effort to remove them stimulated the circulation, for the 'corpse' began to stir and focus her eyes upon him. Terrified, he dropped everything, let out a scream and ran for his life. We can then picture the old lady emerging from her coffin and making her way up the dark steps by the light of the lantern he had obligingly left behind him in his haste. It was a miraculous deliverance from untimely death, but history does not relate whether the scoundrel was thanked or admonished for his actions!

In earlier times, when the leading families in Cornwall vied with each other for supremacy, the ancestors of the Edgcumbes, Bodrugans and Trevanions proudly demonstrated their prowess in war, often for opposing factions. With rivalries, jealousies and a number of old scores to be settled, it was a matter of keeping their wits about them at all times, for brushes with death might occur not only on the field of battle but even on one's own land.

It was just such a situation in 1484, when Sir Richard Edgcumbe, who had been a supporter of Henry, Earl of Richmond (later to become Henry VII) was being hunted down by Richard III's soldiers, led by Sir Henry Trenowth, also known as Henry de Bodrugan. As he heard them approaching, Sir Richard fled from his house and escaped into the woods of Cotehele. With pursuers hot on his trail, he reached an overhanging rock high above the riverbank and realised that he was trapped. In a moment of desperate inspiration, he pulled his cap from his head, cast it into the fast-flowing waters below, clung beneath the precarious overhang and kept very still. The cunning ruse paid off, for finding that the trail had gone cold and seeing the sorry sight of a sodden cap in the swirling waters, Bodrugan and his men assumed that their quarry had slipped into the river and drowned, so they abandoned their search. Sir Richard escaped to France and later returned to erect a chapel on the site of his salvation, as an act of thanksgiving.

The Edgcumbe family's exploits did not stop here, for in the 1760s, an Edgcumbe Countess bored perhaps with cultured company, became a laughing stock by adopting a pig as a close companion, and naming it Cupid. When it died her tears flowed freely, and some subscribed to the theory that an unexplained obelisk erected at around the same time, was established in loving memory. All this proved irresistible to Peter Pindar (John Woolcot), a contemporary satirist, who wrote:

51

'Ode to the Countess of Mount Edgcumbe
On the death of her pet pig Cupid.

Oh! dry those tears so round and big
Nor waste in sighs your precious wind.
Death only takes a little pig,
Your Lord and son are left behind.'

Prima Facie
Murder

WRESTLING and boxing were always very popular in Cornwall, but when it came to brute force and fisticuffs in the early part of the last century, a pugnacious old gipsy known as 'Old Boswell' was a man to be reckoned with. Indeed, his violent temper, power-packed punch and hefty henchmen had helped to earn him the reputation of being the 'King of the Gipsies'. So the grandchild of a man like that would be expected to make his mark in the world. He did; but not quite in the way they had anticipated.

Baby Abraham turned out to be fractious and restless and aggressive by nature, and as he grew to maturity it seemed that these characteristics might be employed to best effect as a recruit in the Duke of Cornwall's Light Infantry. He rather fancied himself in the stylish uniform and he enjoyed the power derived from the use of weaponry. But his downfall came, not in the guise of some hostile bullet on heroic, foreign fields, but as the result of his uncontrollable temper in a peaceful Cornish lane.

In the autumn of 1883, when he was 18 years old, Abraham Boswell, his army career at an ignominious end and now employed as an itinerant chair-mender, met up with a former army mate who was twice his age, in the village of Cubert, a few miles south of Newquay. Thomas Downs, alias Stanley, alias Hugal, was currently in a spot of bother for not paying a fine for drunkenness, but he was basically good humoured.

He was travelling the roads as a razor-grinder which, like chair-mending, is thirsty work, so the two men adjourned to the Hosken Arms, still carrying the tools of their trade. Boswell was feeling disgruntled, but that was not unusual; he was morose by nature, dissatisfied with his lot, and always imagining that people were laughing and sneering at him. In the hope that his companion's humour might mellow after a refreshing draught or two, Downs called to the landlord for a couple of pints, and Boswell said it had better be speedy. As one drink followed another, the disgruntled chair-mender grumbled about the world in general, and chair-mending in particular. His noisy ill-humour radiated across the bar room, much to the discomfort of other folk who had called there for a quiet drink and pleasant chat. Boswell said that he was better off in the army than mending broken chairs and sitting in the pub with the riff-raff here today, and Downs tried to calm him, reminding him gently that his career in the army had not been noted for its happiness and harmony. 'Just 'old yer peace, or yer might be sorry!' warned Boswell, with an evil look in his eye. As he was about to add something even less polite, he caught the eye of the landlord's daughter, Edith, and leered suggestively. But she did not seem to notice. Feeling slighted by this, he deliberately picked a quarrel with Thomas Downs, then moved to a seat on his own and started banging his chair-mending hammer on the table to make sure he was still the centre of attention.

He drained tankard after tankard, loudly smacking his lips, swearing and throwing down the empty receptacles before going onto brandy laced with sugar. If the landlord and his daughter thought of refusing his demands, they would have been brave to thwart him, for things were ominously escalating. Boswell, who was well used to drink, was loud-mouthed and aggressive, but not yet completely intoxicated. Downs, on the other hand, knew when he had drunk enough, and was becoming increasingly concerned about his old mate's behaviour, and feeling some sort of responsibility for it. Any attempts to calm the rising tension met with abuse and only made things worse.

When it came to sharing the payment for the afternoon's drinking session Boswell went wild, kicking Downs in the face and sending the bar-room tables flying in all directions. The very Devil was inside him on that fateful day.

The landlord, backed up by indignant customers, refused to serve him any more drinks, and at length, at about four o'clock, Downs finally persuaded Boswell that enough was enough and led him from the stuffy bar room outside into the fresh, autumn air. 'Ah,' sighed Downs appreciatively, taking deep, calming breaths, ''tis good to be alive, for sure.' But artful Boswell, who was not so intoxicated as he was making out started employing a new range of childish tactics, weaving about in the road and falling over in a contrived fashion, making sure that he did not land on hard stones or in the prickly hedge and letting his friend struggle to pick him up before doing the same thing all over again. As Downs picked up his knife-grinding apparatus and prepared to continue, Boswell let his hat fall to the ground and let his tools scatter for the gratification of seeing his friend trying to retrieve them. Any gentle admonishment was met with shouting, swearing and screaming. This raised the eyebrows of one or two passers-by, which caused Downs to smile apologetically, to ease his embarrassment. 'Who er yer larfin' at?' demanded Boswell, and accused his old mate of making fun of him. 'Calm down, Abbie. Nobody's laughing at you. Come along!' he urged. Passer-by James Tozer, a stone-breaker, appeared on the scene. Without the slightest provocation, Boswell cursed and threatened to 'burst' him. Tozer's automatic response was the only one this bully understood, for he wielded his heavy stone-breaking hammer and effectively put a stop to these antics until he was out of Boswell's sight.

Exactly what happened next will never be known, but Boswell's life was to hang in the balance over how these events would be interpreted. Boswell suddenly pushed Downs into the hedge and knocked him on the head with the chair-mending hammer he had been toying with all afternoon. This was a

55

prelude to a more frenzied attack, which crushed Downs' skull and knocked his brains out. Two boys who saw it happen ran back to the village to get help.

John Bulley, a gardener and a van driver named Chenoweth rushed to the scene to find Boswell still laying into his victim with the hammer, which he was wielding with enormous force. As soon as he became aware of their approach, he casually picked up his weaving canes and strolled off in the direction of Newlyn East, leaving his hat in the road. The two men tried to help the victim, who gasped for breath and almost immediately died. There were pools of blood all over the place, and the heavy, bloodstained hammer lay close to the murdered man's head.

When they were joined by Mr. Cook, an Inland Revenue officer, he agreed to remain at the scene while the other two men tried to apprehend the culprit, assisted shortly afterwards by two more men from the village. The hunted man, who had so nonchalantly departed from the scene of his crime, altered course, but those in pursuit managed to corner him. Even though he was outnumbered, and in a hopeless situation, he did not give up without threats and a struggle. 'Take yer 'ands orf me! I'll kill yer!' he cried. 'I'll kill the lot o' yer! Then I'll fling yer all in the air. There's four o' yer an' only one o' me! Neither you nor forty men could overpower me! I'm the grandson o' Boswell, King o' the Gipsies; I'm someone to be reckoned with!' But they overpowered him, and held him down until PC Hamley arrived on the scene. Realising the situation, the clear-headed villain tried to appear insane, calling out for a pint of ale and a penn'orth of biscuits and cheeses. Then he started to cry and call on God. Then, in a bizarre sequence of events the murderer was placed in a cart beside the mutilated body, which was trundled back to the village. An outhouse of the so recently hospitable Hosken Arms then became a temporary mortuary until a post mortem was conducted by Mr. Vigurs, a surgeon. Meanwhile, Boswell was taken into custody at St Columb.

An inquest was held in the schoolroom at Cubert, upon the body of Thomas Downs, itinerant tinker, found murdered on the highway, and Boswell was taken before the magistrates at St Columb and committed to trial at the Cornwall & Devon Assizes in Exeter. It was fully expected that Boswell's violent life was to end with a walk to the gallows.

However, Abraham Boswell was to meet with a small measure of luck. At the trial he was indicted for the wilful murder of Thomas Hugo Downs at Cubert on October 2nd. The evidence was the same as that given at the inquest, but the learned counsel stated that if the jury could by any possibility reduce the crime to anything short of murder they would, of course, do so. In the *Royal Cornwall Gazette* it was reported:

'The defence counsel having called witnesses as to character addressed the jury for the defence. The prisoner was a mere lad, not yet 19, and up to the present time had borne as good a character as possible. They had not before them a man with a long, black record of crime against him. Therefore, he asked them to start with a favourable impression of the lad, and to hesitate before they said he could be guilty of so fearful a crime as murder. It would be impossible, and it would be an insult to them and to the judge, for him to attempt to deny the facts of this most painful case. As regarded the facts he and his learned friend who had so fairly and temperately conducted the case for the prosecution were at one. There could be no doubt that on that afternoon of October the prisoner had a serious quarrel with the unfortunate deceased, they got drunk together, and by the hand of the prisoner the unfortunate man lost his life. But the law in its mercy allowed the jury, if they thought the evidence justified it, to return the alternative verdict of manslaughter, and against that verdict he should not have a word to say. That these two men quarrelled and were drunk there could be no doubt, and on these grounds he asked them to reduce the crime to one of manslaughter, for which he ventured to remind them the law provided the most terrible punishment that could be awarded short of death.'

57

His Lordship, in summing up, said the jury might, if the circumstances admitted it, consider whether that which was prima facie murder, that is, murder at first sight, might not be reduced to manslaughter. As to the disputed points of the case, first they had to consider whether the prisoner was in a state of intoxication or not. This was always very difficult to say, because witnesses were so loath to tell exactly the truth, and some persons were loath to admit that anyone was the worse for drink, but at all events these two men must have been drinking in the Hosken Arms for over two hours. Drink was no excuse for crime; a man could not put an enemy into his own mouth to steal away his brains and then plead that as an excuse, but he would tell them why they might look at the question of drink in this case. A drunken man was answerable by his life if he killed another, but if the jury should think the prisoner and the deceased had a quarrel in that five minutes which Mr. Bulley said elapsed between the time they left the house and the time his attention was again called to them by a boy, if there was a quarrel in that time and the deceased had struck the prisoner, and that then the prisoner, overcome by passion and his blood excited by the blow he got from the deceased, struck him with a hammer, that would justify the jury in reducing the offence to manslaughter. They must consider that fairly. There was no evidence of what took place during that five minutes. Words, however provoking, would not justify them in reducing the charge; but if there had been a blow, and they should see evidence to warrant the conclusion that the deceased had retaliated with a blow, and that then the prisoner had used the hammer and had killed him, that might justify the jury in saying it was manslaughter.

The jury took ten minutes to return a verdict of manslaughter, and Abraham Boswell was sentenced to penal servitude for 20 years.

The Wreck
of the
New Commercial

'ASK not, Sailor, whose body lies here. I wish you better luck than mine, and a kindlier sea', quoth the ancient proverb. It could apply to any number of victims of shipwreck, resting in many a coastal Cornish churchyard. But the price paid by one of them led to something positive in the heroic cause of preserving life from shipwreck. This was no rough, tough, rumbustious Jolly Jack Tar, but the sedate fourth daughter of a genteel north country parson, who married a sea captain, and became a central character in an epic tale of heroism and tragedy which brought recognition and glory, but most importantly, the establishment of a lifeboat station at Sennen Cove.

The coast around Land's End, with its rocks and reefs, conflicting tides and currents has long been notorious with seafarers the world over, and in days of sail the area accounted for a colossal catalogue of shipwrecks. A large percentage of these fell victim to the grand and fearful Brisons, twin rocks which jut defiantly above the waves a mile or so to the south west of Cape Cornwall. The name 'Breson' or 'Breezon' was thought to signify a cruel, sharp reef. They were also known locally as The Sisters. Even on the calmest of summer days,

the waters cream and foam and swell around these menacing obstacles as if in deference.

The brig *New Commercial* of Whitby, of 250 tons burthen had left Liverpool and was bound for the Spanish Main, under the command of Captain Sanderson, early in January 1851. His wife, who had joined him for the voyage, was pleased to be with him, and excited at the prospect of seeing some of the fascinating places he had told her about. But the brig was proving to be rather too lively for comfort when they suddenly ran into a thick blanket of fog. This was a combination of dangers all too well known to local mariners. The seas were running high, and the vessel was bouncing along with the wind in her tail, her sails full-billowing. Then suddenly a panic-stricken cry rang out above the roar of wind and wave and flapping canvas, 'Breakers ahead!' Almost instantly they struck the reef between the Brisons with such force and crash that masts snapped and timbers split and humanity was flung to the elements. By some miracle the eight crewmen, the Captain and his wife managed to scramble onto a rocky ledge, but their ship disintegrated with the relentless force of those mighty waves. This cruel coast had claimed another vessel. How many of its frightened, shipwrecked victims huddling together on the rock would it hasten to the sailors' heaven, Fiddler's Green, on this occasion?

To those perched precariously on the wet rocks, mesmerised by shock and bewildering circumstances, it seemed as if those hungry waves were tantalising them. The angry, playful seas rose forth, splattering, teasing and threatening to engulf them, before retreating, and repeating the performance. It happened again and again. But the victims of the shipwreck were resolute; for the rest of that day and throughout that night they clung there. Mary thought of her family and the serene vicarage back home, and she prayed. Little did her loved ones know how she was spending the early hours of this Sabbath. The crewmen faced the ordeal with stolid stoicism, wondering whether they would ever see their wives and sweethearts again. That chilling, spraydrenched, terrifying night on the rock seemed never-ending. Would they ever see the dawn? The storm intensified, and the waves reached higher and higher. Soaked, cold, hungry and dehydrated, they tried to tighten their grip, and hang on as best they could. In this terrifying, unaccustomed situation it was steadying to turn their minds to everyday things, and make a promise that if they survived this ordeal, they would give heartfelt thanks for each remaining day, and never take anything for granted again.

After a time some began to lose their concentration, and others became more fatalistic. Then came one enormous wave which swept them all off the rock. Their heartrending screams mingled with the cacophany of wind and wave; the screams subsided, but only three had been granted a second deliverance from a watery grave.

A half caste seaman called Isaac Williams was able to scramble onto a section of floating spar. Using a plank for a paddle and a piece of torn canvas for a sail, he bravely set forth into the darkness. It is at times like this that people manage to achieve the seemingly impossible, for this futile attempt actually paid off. He was spotted from the Sennen shore at dawn, and rescued by some fishermen who had bravely launched through the treacherous breakers to reach him. Meanwhile, the other two survivors, Captain Sanderson and his wife, had been thrown up on the Little Brison.

News of those in peril travelled fast. Captain George Davies, who was Inspecting Commander of the Coastguard at Penzance ordered the revenue cutter *Sylvia* to the scene, while he and local colleagues took up positions on Cape Cornwall. The *Sylvia*, under the command of Mr. Forward, battled her way gallantly around the Land's End through angry waves and swirling seas, which lifted them up then plunged them into deep troughs, sending them hither and thither amidst flying spume and spray. It must have been a heartening moment for the two castaways, when they realised that help was on its way. On coming abreast of Cape Cornwall, Mr. Forward launched one of the cutter's small boats, and made repeated attempts with four of his crew to reach the rock. But they had to return to their ship after prolonged efforts, because of the ferocity of the sea. They remained on stand-by as increasing numbers of sightseers gathered on the lofty promontory. The hours dragged by, and as darkness was falling, Mr. Forward hoisted his colours and hove-to, in order to give some encouragement to the unfortunate couple on the rock, who were now realising that they would have to endure another night. But now, as darkness fell, they were heartened by the close proximity of the cutter, and its reassuring light.

Monday morning seemed an eternity in coming, but by the time it did the wind had veered a little to the south east, and the seas had moderated. Hundreds of people gathered along the shore as the morning wore on, and the sun shafted through the cloudiness, throwing a spotlight on the central figures of the drama, pitiful and cowering on the rock, surrounded by a heaving, silvery sea. By one o'clock three boats manned by fishermen and a fourth by coastguards were on their way from Sennen Cove, while Captain Davies was approaching in a preventive boat from Pendeen. Mr. Forward was proceeding centre stage in the cutter's boat. They were encouraged by cheers from the ever increasing throng of people on the shore. But the seas were running so high that no boat could venture within a 100 yards of the Brisons. The shipwrecked victims could never survive another night on the exposed rock, so the only alternative means of rescue in such a situation was then resorted to.

This was in the nature of a trial experiment, for the nine-pounder Dennett rockets which Captain Davies had brought along in the preventive boat had never been put to the test here, either at sea or from the shore. And furthermore the instructions specifically stated that the person firing them should be positioned several feet to the rear to avoid danger. This was impossible in the circumstances. One of the men, Gunner Selley, bravely volunteered, but Captain Davies was not the sort of man to place another in a situation like this. So he ordered his crew to board a Sennen boat, anchored within 100 yards of the rock, placed another boat astern, fixed the triangular frame into position, and fired. For a moment he was surrounded by a sheet of flame, caused by the back-fire, but luckily he escaped injury. Unfortunately the line caught on a sharp edge of rock, severed, and descended into the swirling seas. The couple on the rocks were dismayed, and the sound of mass disappointment rose from the onlookers across the water. There was a poignant quietness as preparations were made to fire a second line. The Sandersons waited with bated breath. Then a mighty cheer rang out from the shore as the line reached the rock, and landed close to Captain Sanderson. A sudden sunbeam lit the scene, as his wife clasped her hands in thankfulness to heaven. Some say that this devoted wife wanted her beloved husband to be carried to safety first, but he insisted on fastening a line around her waist, and gently encouraged the frightened woman to make her leap for freedom.

All eyes were on this slight figure as she stood poised for the jump. But when she found the nerve to do so, she chose the wrong moment, for it coincided with a succession of three mountainous waves, which rose mightily, placing them all in peril. Indeed, the boats disappeared from view for quite some time, and the cry rang out from the horrified watchers on the shore, 'They are gone! They are gone!' The momentous waves passed on, and those involved in the drama became visible once more. Mary Sanderson, who had taken a terrible battering was drawn, still breathing, from the water, but was so exhausted from the extended ordeal that her life was at its lowest ebb. Despite the care and kindness of her rescuers, who covered her with their clothes and tried to revive her, this courageous woman who had endured so much and shown such spirit in the most testing of circumstances, died before the boat reached the shore. Her husband was saved with a line from another boat and landed at Sennen Cove, where he was attended by Mr. Quick, a surgeon of St Just, and by Mrs Maxey of the coastguard station, who had also cared for fellow survivor, Isaac Williams.

This epic rescue brought much recognition and glory to the isolated little fishing village at Sennen Cove, capable of providing any number of first class fishermen to man the lifeboat which arrived shortly afterwards. Prestigious medals and monetary awards were made to all who took part in it. Captain George Davies, who had already been accorded much recognition for being personally involved in the saving of hundreds of lives received a gold medal of the RNLI and many other awards, and was appointed Inspector of Lifeboats shortly afterwards.

Mary Sanderson was buried in Sennen churchyard and her tombstone sombrely reminds us that 'In the midst of life we are in death'.

'Send her to Temple Moors'

THE red crosses on the stained glass windows of Temple church recall a rich and colourful past. Though it is set in an apparent backwater, this place has seen its full share of sophistication, corruption and degradation in an 800 year old history.

The forgotten little hamlet of Temple lies in the heart of Bodmin Moor and recalls in its name the area's former connections with the Knights Templar, a military and religious order, established in the 12th century, at the time of the Crusades. The lands around Temple were situated in an area yielding tin and were regarded as highly desirable, with great potential. The streaming of tin (filtering and extracting from streams and waterways) had been a flourishing industry in Cornwall since the Bronze Age, exploited by a succession of outsiders. The Knights Templar figured among those who employed cheap labour and grew rich on the proceeds and, having acquired these lands, they set about establishing a church and instilling decent Christian standards into the primitive moorland folk as well as offering a welcome haven for weary travellers. There was an inter-linking network of these religious foundations throughout Europe. Irish pilgrims were thought to have sailed up the Camel estuary to Padstow and gone overland to the premier port on the Fowey river, rather than risk the dangerous sea passage around Land's End, and a host of other pilgrims passed this way.

On the dissolution of the Knights Templar in 1312, Capella de Templo, as it was then known, was taken over by the rivalling Knights Hospitallers, who had a preceptory at Trebighe in St Ive on the south eastern fringes of the moor.

Capella de Templo was a little world of its own, far removed from its Cornish environment and the lives of the moorland folk, who worked hard as the seasons dictated, and lived simply. In sharp contrast, the preceptory was a place of sophistication with good communications, where people came and went bringing news from afar. It had a structured, disciplined hierarchy, with two grades of serving men. The high class servants, or 'generosi' were gentlemen who enjoyed the privilege of wearing stylish uniforms and coat armour, and were notoriously disdainful of the free servants who merely attended to the mundane duties of the household.

When the Hospitallers' church at Temple was dissolved in the 18th century, it became part of the diocese of Exeter, but escaped the usual visitations of the Bishop. In the absence of such supervision the place became a law unto itself, geared to the convenience and desires of its incumbents in this misty, moorland setting. All sorts of irregularities began to creep in, and the place gained such notoriety that it found a niche in colloquial language. 'Send her to Temple Moors!' became a cutting, witty remark to be made about dubious women, calculated to raise a smile, and demolish a reputation. For in their efforts to swell the coffers of this run down establishment serving an impoverished community, the clergy took it upon themselves to perform marriages without banns or licence, gaining the reputation of being the 'Gretna Green of Bodmin Moor', attracting eloping couples, passing worshippers and the general hoi polloi. Their unconventional approach struck a note of empathy with outcasts, villains, rebels and others on the edge of society. Unmarried mothers came to have their babies here, and suicides were granted burial here. Where else could such people look for help and refuge?

It could not last. The church's irregularities came to the attention of the diocese and normal diocesan practices and discipline were enforced. The revenue from eloping lovers, former illegal activities, and passing worshippers who dropped in to satisfy their curiosity, died away, and Temple church fell into a state of neglect. Strangely symbolic was the fact that an ash seedling took root amid the picturesque ruins, for in folklore the ash tree was considered lucky with powers of healing.

Perhaps the ash tree fulfilled its promise, for the church was destined to rise again. In the middle of the 19th century a service was held amidst the romantic ruins as a prelude to raising funds for it to be rebuilt on the foundations of that early church of the Knights Templar. It was officially opened and dedicated to St Catherine in May 1883 by Dr Benson, the Bishop of Truro, who later became the Archbishop of Canterbury.

The wheel of fortune has turned to leave this once busy hamlet in a backwater loop off today's busy A30, while pilgrims of a very different kind traverse the fast and furious highway, little dreaming of those colourful days of long ago.

Smugglers, Wreckers and Privateers

PRUSSIA Cove, to the east of Marazion has been the hub of some of the most amazing feats of daring ever carried out by smugglers in this country. Formerly known as Porth Leah or the King's Cove, its present name recalls those swashbuckling exploits, for the notorious John Carter, landlord of the local inn, known to one and all as the 'King of Prussia' and his family monopolised most of the smuggling and privateering trade in the west, using this cove as the centre of operations. He created a harbour and connecting road and converted the caves into cellars for smuggled goods. Not wishing to be subject to unwelcome visitors, he constructed and mounted a formidable cliff-top battery and he had the audacity to engage in fire approaching revenue cutters intent on investigating his activities. He also indulged in an on-going battle of wits with the customs officers of Penzance, which he obviously relished.

The story goes that once, while he was on business elsewhere, excisemen paid the cove a visit and seized a consignment, newly arrived from France, which they placed in their Custom House store. On returning and learning about these events, he made arrangements for the store to be raided and his ill-gotten gains recovered, roundly declaring that he had promised his customers delivery of the goods and his integrity was at stake. In his own way, he was an honourable man, and when the officers discovered that the store had been broken into they were confident that he had left the rest intact, knowing that he would never touch anything not rightfully his.

The Carter family's smuggling activities prospered in the second part of the 18th century, developing useful contacts in high places, and becoming more sophisticated and ambitious as the War of American Independence opened up more opportunities to combine smuggling with privateering. They indulged in many a daring skirmish and found themselves caught up with international events, with time spent languishing in prison. Taking his cutter to St Malo for repairs, John's brother Harry was arrested for not carrying proper documentation, and deemed a pirate. John went to rescue Harry and was himself arrested. But their high-flown friends came in useful; through the intervention of the Lords of the Admiralty, both were exchanged for Frenchmen. Whatever setbacks they encountered, they had a happy knack of bouncing back.

When it came to ruffians and rogues it would be hard to beat the excesses of the Breage and Germoe fraternity whose wrecking activities were so brutal that vulnerable mariners would fervently pray:

'God keep us from rocks and shelving sands
And save us from Breage and Germoe men's hands.'

Some say that ships were deliberately lured onto the cruel rocks by such artful means as the emplacement of false lights, which were sometimes attached to cattle and donkeys on the clifftops, whose random meanderings might create the illusion of vessels wallowing in the waves. Some say that survivors were beaten to death.

Chilling tales were told of the ruthless and compelling Coppinger, better known as 'Cruel Coppinger', who operated around the shores of north Devon and Cornwall after making an unscheduled appearance in these parts as the sole survivor of a shipwreck. Having made a stylish entrance through the raging surf during a fearful storm, he is said to have ripped a cloak from an old woman's back, placed it around his own shoulders and leapt up on a horse being ridden by a rich man's daughter. She took him to her father's house where he was kindly received and given food and clothing. The villain, knowing that he was on to a good thing, charmed and won the hand of the young heiress, which gave him access to her father's extensive lands and riches when he conveniently died shortly afterwards. The new bride soon discovered that life with her handsome, dashing husband was not a bed of roses; a situation which grew worse when the only child of this unhappy union turned out to be a flinty chip off the old block, terrorising and blackmailing the local children.

Cruel Coppinger was the sort of villain who gathered weaker characters around him, then retreated while others did his dirty work and took the blame. He enlisted the services of an ill-assorted gang of smugglers and trained them to his ways. He acquired a speedy sailing ship, known as the *Black Prince,* which was crewed by a motley bunch gathered from the streets by the less-than-gentle persuasion of his press gang louts. In his career of smuggling, wrecking and plundering, cruelty was his creed and swashbuckling his style. When situations got too tight he invariably made a hurried departure on his trusty stallion.

When it came to paying the final price for a lengthy catalogue of evil deeds, Cruel Coppinger decided it was time to quit. It was almost as if his mis-spent career of greed, violence and murder along this northern coast had turned full circle, for he escaped the perils of remaining on land by escaping to sea at the height of a violent storm. The lightning cracked and the thunder rolled, but it seems that the Devil looked after his own. As soon as Cruel Coppinger had boarded the vessel which awaited him, she seemed to fade away like a phantom ship. And local folk who now slept more easily in their beds at night would tell their children:

71

'Will you hear of the cruel Coppinger?
He came from a foreign kind;
He was brought to us by the salt water,
He was carried away by the wind.'

Au Fait
with the Fairies

IN the 17th century, there was a widespread belief in Cornwall's unique brand of little sprites, which included piskie pranksters, caring brownies, the playful and occasionally helpful fairies, troublesome spriggans and the restless buccas or knockers thought to haunt the mines. All were regarded as spirits of the long departed, suspended somewhere between heaven and hell, and whether they were a help or a hindrance, it paid to keep on the right side of them if possible. So when a 19 year old labourer's daughter from St Teath claimed to enjoy communion with the fairies it raised fewer eyebrows than such an occurence would do today. Indeed, it was taken so seriously that she was thrown into prison and subjected to the most horrifying of conditions.

It all began in 1645, when Anne Jefferies, who was in service to the local worthy Mr. Moses Pitt, had a powerful vision in which she saw fairies. Mr. Pitt, who found her in a collapsed state in the garden, said that she was so frightened by the encounter with the little people that it caused a convulsive fit. The fairies, it seems, were coy about making their presence known to other mortals, for after Anne had been carried into the house she opened her eyes and exclaimed, 'There they are! There they are – just gone out of the window! Did you see them? Did you see them?' But no one else ever saw them. This was a prelude to a lifelong association with the helpful fairies,

reputedly bringing Anne not only the rare gift of clairvoyance and the miraculous powers of healing, but the ability to become invisible at will.

As soon as Anne recovered she made her way to the church. Her life was transformed; she became very devout and spent much of her time preaching, healing the sick and foretelling the future. After curing her mistress of a serious malady, word spread until people from all over the countryside, young and old, rich and poor, with all manner of ills, flocked to her door in hopes of a cure. These were effected by the laying on of hands, and the use of wondrous potions and salves secretly supplied by the fairies. Mr. Pitt, who recorded some of these amazing events, marvelled about some of the mysterious happenings around him. He described her dancing in the garden with invisible partners, and most incredibly, disappearing and re-appearing.

The fairies not only supplied magical medicines, they also brought her daily bread, which Moses Pitt, who once had the chance to sample some, declared to be wonderful, the finest he had ever tasted. Her favourite delicacies were sweetened almonds and sweetmeats, which, she claimed, were carried to her by the wee folk clad in green, or occasionally by the birds of the air. The fay folk, who competed with each other in efforts to please, even once brought her a silver cup as a gift for a small child she dearly loved. Perhaps it was her vision of the future that compelled her to reject the food of mortals, as she termed it, from 'harvest time 'till Yuletide' one year, for the experience was to stand her in good stead throughout the dark and cruel times which awaited her. When it came to Christmas time she joined her host and his family at the table for traditional Christmas fare, out of courtesy towards them.

Anne's well known ability to see into the future, and her boldness in commenting on events which might be construed as political, gave rise to apprehension and enmity in some quarters, and accusations of being a witch. Certain ministers and magistrates had tried to convince her that her fairies were evil spirits, and urged her to reject them. While seated at the dining table with the Pitt family one day, she was summoned thrice by fairy calling, and begged permission to leave the room. When she returned, she was in a state of agitation, for her fairy friends had become aware that people were trying to turn her against them. They were deeply hurt, and had given her some strange advice. When the time was right she was to quote the First Epistle of St John, Chapter IV, verse 1.

The evil, notorious John Tregeagle, steward to the Earl of Radnor and a Justice of the Peace, sent a warrant for Anne's arrest, accusing her of witchcraft and communing with the devil, and had her cast into Bodmin Gaol, cruelly instructing that she should not be fed. Despite being deprived of food and ill-treated in terrible conditions, Anne amazed everyone with her healthy appearance and general demeanour, for the fairies had been true to their word, keeping her cheerful company and supplying her with goodly fare. The accusations could not be upheld, for though illiterate, she proved devout and extremely well versed in the scriptures, and her interrogators were dumbfounded when she opened her Bible to reveal a text which just fitted the bill. It read: 'Dearly beloved, believe not every spirit, but try the spirits whether they be of God'. They became even more disconcerted when she calmly told them that nothing they might do could ever hurt her, and suggested that they might be wiser not to meddle any further. She was discharged from prison, but kept under guard in the town by the wicked Tregeagle whose evil exploits were to earn him an unenviable place in folklore as the Cornish bogeyman, who sold his soul to the Devil.

The case was eventually dismissed through lack of evidence, and Anne emerged from her long ordeal looking healthy and radiant. She spent some time in service in a household near Padstow, where she continued her healing mission, and met and married one William Warren. There were many who sought to discover the nature of her mysterious powers. Moses Pitt, the son of Anne's old master and mistress, who was a boy when she had entered service in his household at the age of 19, wanted the strange events surrounding her to be documented. There was a letter concerning her in the Clarendon Manuscripts in 1647, and in 1696 he wrote a printed letter to the Lord Bishop of Gloucester giving an account of his early memories of Anne Jefferies and of her later life. As his statement needed some verification and he was working as a printer in London at the time, he asked his old friend Humphrey Martin, father of the child who had received the gift of a silver goblet, to carry out an independent investigation, hoping that Anne might be prevailed upon to reveal her strange secret at last to satisfy the curiosity of mankind. But Anne steadfastly refused to divulge any details of her relationship with the fairies. 'I will not tell 'ee. I will tell no one. I woulds't not even tell my own father my secret, if 'e were still alive.' 'Prithee, why not?' enquired Mr. Martin. 'Why, if I was ter tell 'ee, the word would spread around, and folks would make up books and ballads. I do not want my name in books and ballads. I would not tell anyone my secret,' she declared, 'not even for five 'undred pound!'

Anne Jefferies lived to a ripe old age and took her secret with her to the grave.

Hurling Heroes

THE stone circles known as The Hurlers on Bodmin Moor in the parish of St Cleer may intrigue the archaeologist and appeal to the romantic, but they also recall a unique and rugged Cornish sport rooted in antiquity. For the story goes that a team of sportsmen enjoying a hearty game of hurling were turned to stone for profaning the Sabbath, and thus remain in petrified attitudes of joyful play for eternity. The notion of such harsh divine intervention seems strange in view of the fact that this popular game, with its idealistic, sporting motto 'Guare wheag, yu guare teag' (Fair play is good play) was traditionally played on the Sabbath, usually after the Town Feast. (This was Saint's Day, the special day of the patron saint of the town church, when prayer and processions were followed by feasting, fun and games.)

The rules of Hurling were very loose, and the game, played with a silver ball, could take place in the town or over the wild, open countryside. It was rather like rugby, with appointed goalposts but without referee or whistle and it tended to become a rough, tough, free for all, which undoubtedly helped to sort the men out from the boys.

Hurling was a sport for everyone, rather than for an elite. It could be played anywhere as a full-blooded spectator sport in which injuries and battlescars were bravely borne and subsequently exhibited with pride. But it was not merely a game; it had a much deeper significance. It may well be of Pagan origin, and some say the tossing of the silver ball symbolises the rivalry between summer and winter, with the airborne silver ball representing the sun. Many saw the silver ball as an omen, and would seek some means of touching it for good luck. By the same token the winning of the trophy augured well for the community for the following year. Young and old and folk of every situation would turn out to support the cream of their local manhood, anxious to demonstrate its supremacy over rivalling towns, villages or parishes. Sometimes it was a case of married men taking on the bachelors to create some fun and excitement, or, as in St Ives, it could be the Toms, Williams and Johns taking on men with other first names; a system which worked while parents obligingly chose the right mix of names for their baby boys. Hurling could be played through the streets, as was traditional at St Columb. The shops and vulnerable buildings prepared for the blitz, and spectators could watch from windows and convenient vantage points along the way. Or the hurling could take to the country, covering a much wider area. Part of the skill across fields, hedgerows, ditches, bogs, ponds, rivers and bridges, was employing artful tactics, and taking the opposition by surprise. This was more demanding for the spectators, who were obliged to dash around to keep abreast of the action, rather than being content with sounds and distant echoes across the countryside.

To be a good hurler one needed to take a cue from nature. It helped to be able to run like a hare, leap like a deer, climb like a cat, hide like a rabbit and employ the cunning of a fox. It was similarly useful to have perfect ball control, to be able to box and wrestle like a champion; to have foresight in the avoiding of tight situations, and the ability to extricate oneself from potentially lethal ones. Some, who lacked such sterling qualities sustained wounds, became maimed for life, or even died from mortal injuries received during the course of this fun-loving pursuit. Nevertheless, this sport of heroes, with its regional variations, mellowed considerably since the 17th century, when the historian Carew described it as being 'a play both rude and rough'. Scores of players took part and the contest began with the gleaming, silver ball being tossed high into the air. There was tremendous competition to catch it, and the player who succeeded in doing so would grip hold of it tightly, and take off like the wind in the direction of his goal with the opposing pack hot on his heels. At just the right moment he would 'sky' the ball, and whoever caught it would become the new object of attention for the eager pack, endeavouring to trip him up and bury him beneath a writhing mass of humanity, punching, kicking and wrestling, until someone else got the ball and became the centre of attention. And so it went on, over hill and dale and through the thicket and mire; all good, clean fun, and if things got a bit foul, some gentlemanly player, no doubt, would point it out with the greatest courtesy, and everyone would sportingly agree that 'fair play is good play', and nobody would argue with the referee, because there was no referee.

The object of the exercise was to touch the ball down inside the goal, and the winners were the side which had scored the most goals before someone impartially decided to declare the game at an end. There would be hearty cheers, glee, elation, disappointment and disillusionment as the battered, mud spattered players made their excitable way to some kind of celebration, laughing, shouting, bantering, arguing and moaning and making silly jokes and jibes. In the country they would often be welcomed by a member of the local gentry, where the precious silver coated ball (after a good scrub, one hopes) was submersed in a great tankard of beer, which was then distributed to the thirsty players. The captain of the winning side would proudly accept the silver trophy, to be placed in a proud and prominent place until the following year.

The
Mystery of
Pengersick Castle

MYSTERY and legend have always surrounded Pengersick Castle, near the shores of Mount's Bay, originally constructed in the days of Henry VIII, with imposing battlements and two fine towers commanding views across the water. For this impressive pile, occupied by a succession of wealthy folk who set themselves apart from ordinary people, was an enigma to the impoverished, close-knit community of fisherfolk, miners and smugglers, and its history is confused and unclear.

It seems that one inhabitant, the Pengersick who gave the place its name, was a nouveau riche, and something of a social climber, for he thought he might be accepted into the local gentry if he could persuade his son to marry an ageing lady of high birth who had an all-consuming passion for the handsome young man. For her part, this fading beauty who was experiencing lean times had a desire to share his wealth, as well as his life. She made repeated attempts to beguile him, and even employed the celebrated witch of Fraddam to concoct love potions; but all to no avail. In desperation, to achieve a closer daily presence with him, she married his father and employed the witch's daughter Bitha to act on her behalf and continue administering the secret spells to the son. The delicate situation backfired on her, for Bitha fell hopelessly in love with him too. So the new mistress of Pengersick made even more determined efforts to seduce the young man and when he rejected her, unrequited love turned to hate and engendered a desire for revenge. She confined herself in one of the towers, giving her husband to understand that she was with child, and that she was seeking refuge from his son's violent passion for her. Incensed and outraged, the Lord of Pengersick agreed that his only son was a knave and a villain; fit only to be sold into slavery, and readily joined in a plot for him to be carried off by a band of pirates.

Their wicked plot was successful, but the young man's departure left an aching void in his stepmother's scheming heart, which became filled with the desire to do away with the old man and acquire all his lands and wealth. In doing so she again harnessed the powers of the witch's daughter, who guided her in the blending of strange concoctions to bring about a slow and painful death through poisoning. It was only on his deathbed that the naive old fool, still blinded by his snobbery, learnt the truth about his ruthless wife from Bitha and realised that he was being poisoned. It is said that the wicked woman, now a widow, withered away in the tower, deformed and grotesque through handling so much poison, and too ashamed to show herself.

Many years later the young Lord of Pengersick returned from the East, bringing with him an oriental bride, who was not only beautiful, but also an accomplished musician. He had left by sea and returned on horseback, with his retinue in attendance. In the intervening years he had developed an interest in the occult and allied Eastern arts. Having re-established himself at Pengersick, most of his days were spent in his lonely chamber making spells, uttering strange incantations in foreign tongues and producing multicoloured smoke and amazing varieties of strange odours which wafted through the open windows and across the countryside, permeating the air for miles around.

Thus local folk caught a pungent whiff of curious goings-on. No one was allowed inside those mysterious walls, and the handful of carefully chosen servants who had arrived with him were sworn to secrecy on pain of death.

What the locals did not know, they speculated about and weird and wonderful stories were passed around. It was said that on stormy nights the master could be heard calling up the spirits, and his terrified servants would rush out as the place filled up with demons, who artfully schemed and connived to get the better of the enchanter. But when things got too difficult for him to cope with, the dark eyed beauty only had to pluck a few sweet notes on her lyrical harp for the spirits to flee through the air in terror, shrieking and whining above the fearsome sound of the storm. All became sweetness and light as the servants ventured back again, re-assured by their gentle mistress. If this situation was mysterious and bizarre, folk became accustomed to it, and to the prosperity their ample wealth had brought to this impoverished community, for they kept a good table and spent their money freely in the local markets. But things became decidedly more uneasy after the appearance of an unidentified stranger from the Orient, who moved stealthily around, spoke to no one and was wont to venture out along the shore at night. If it had been eerie when the incantations, sweet music and emissions of weird coloured, strange-scented smoke had filled the air, it was decidedly more so when it stopped, and expectation hung heavily upon the silent air.

Then, one dark and stormy night it happened. A sudden glow in the sky was the first indication that something was amiss. Within moments the whole area was illuminated in fearful splendour as Pengersick Castle went up in flames. Shouts and screams and agonised cries rent the air and the faithful servants fled for their lives as the angry flames licked here and there and everywhere and huge sections of masonry toppled to the ground. But what had become of the young Lord and his lady? If their arrival had been strange and unexpected, this was nothing compared with the manner of their departure. For the story goes that as the fire reached its awesome height, the forms of Pengersick, his lady and the stranger arose from the heart of the flames, hovered momentarily above those crumbling walls, then shot to Eternity in a searing blaze of light.

Harpies in
Human Form

IN the days of sail, March and October, around the time of the Equinox, were notorious times for shipwreck here, and October 1846 brought one of the most severe gales that the northern coast of Cornwall had ever experienced, resulting in more casualties between Newquay and Hartland than anyone could remember. One of the victims of this prolonged storm was the splendid barquentine *Samaritan*, outward bound from Liverpool for Constantinople, with a valuable mixed cargo including bale goods. She struck Park Head, between Newquay and Padstow and was driven ashore at Bedruthan Steps, and having lost eight of her crew of ten she was dashed to pieces, with her cargo scattered all over the shore.

An excited throng of wreckers had already reached the beach by the following morning, which dawned clear and bright. They had clambered down the steep, precarious steps, fashioned some say by smugglers for the convenient handling of their illicit consignments regularly landed here. It was an unholy scene of greed and cruel destruction with determined looters rushing around, screaming, squabbling and snatching up whatever they could lay their hands upon. As if to add more poignancy to the God-forsaken situation, expensive silks and cottons and trappings of sophistication which had broken open from their iron-bound bales lay sodden in the sand and seaweed, while shreds of finery adorned the rocks and fluttered furiously from their sharp edges.

As news of the rich pickings spread, hundreds more flocked to the scene from the surrounding countryside, while customs officers, coastguards and the agent from Lloyds made frantic attempts to restrain the lawless mob, intent on plundering the wreck. Many arrests were made; indeed, it was said that Bodmin Gaol was bulging with the miscreants. It was also said that the womenfolk of the area flaunted themselves in their unaccustomed finery for months afterwards. It was to become one of Cornwall's most notorious cases of wrecking, and the women proved to be the worst offenders. Hundreds of them flocked here wearing long cloaks to conceal the goods they so boldly claimed and carried off. Any attempts at concealment were abandoned when they reached the country lanes, where they giggled merrily and bragged the rest of the way home. However, a number of these brazen 'harpies in human form', had the smiles wiped from their faces when houses were searched and they received their cumuppance. But the excisemen were not so smart when they called at one isolated farmhouse where they were refused permission to search the marital bedroom on account of the wife's imminent confinement. Had they pressed the point and peered under the bed, they would have found a host of receptacles – apart from the one with a handle.

Perhaps the most comprehensive coup of all was carried out by George Lee, an ex-Naval man who had form as a local wrecker, and who operated with a dupe called Northcott. Somehow they always seemed to get a lucky break, and this was no exception, for while others were congratulating themselves on making off with mere silk and cotton finery, Lee and Northcott stumbled on the contents of the ship's safe, which they quietly stuffed into their pockets. So far, so good. But those over-zealous preventive men were swarming around the shore and surrounding countryside and carrying out inspections at the foot of the steps. The challenge was how to get the money away from the scene without getting caught. Northcott broke

out into a cold sweat at the very thought of ending up in prison, so Lee unselfishly offered to shoulder all the risk. It was well known that Northcott was his usual accomplice, and therefore under suspicion, but on this occasion he would carry all the gold coins in his pockets and Northcott, who would leave the beach sometime later would be found to have nothing on him if searched. They would make their separate ways home, and Lee would deliver his partner's share later in the day. So they split up and Lee was able to divert any official's attentions away from his pockets by feigning reluctance at relinquishing some bulky goods concealed beneath his jacket. He walked on, and hoped that the coins in his pockets would not chink and give the game away as he climbed the steep steps. Northcott, on the other hand, who had nothing to incriminate him, daydreamed about what he would do with all the money as he helped a loaded Harpy up the hazardous cliff stepway.

Back home, the old grandfather clock in Northcott's kitchen chimed away the hours. Where was Lee? What could have happened? Had he been caught? Would he, Northcott, be implicated? Grim visions of Bodmin Gaol floated before him. Then to his relief he heard the sound of approaching footsteps, and rushed to the door, where he found Lee, battered and bloodstained, blurting out a story about being attacked and robbed by scoundrels, and there being no honour among the great fraternity these days. Why, his very pockets had been cut clean away, and he plaintively put his hands in the gap where the pockets had been and twiddled his fingers to reinforce the fact that there was nothing left to share. The faithful accomplice accepted the story, and sympathised with his plight. But not long afterwards, George Lee became the proud owner of a fine new cottage standing in its own land.

The wrecking of the *Samaritan* found immortality in this little rhyme:

'The good *Samaritan* came ashore
To feed the hungry and clothe the poor,
Barrels of beef and bales of linen,
No poor man shall want a shillin.'

A
Leading Spirit
of His Age

SIR Humphry Davy, the most prestigious son of Penzance, philosopher, scientist and man of many talents who achieved worldwide acclaim, was best remembered around these parts for having invented the miners' lamp, and was regarded as the miners' unofficial patron saint. This local lad who made good was born in Market Jew Street on 17th December, 1778, into the family of Robert Davy, a carver and gilder and his wife Grace, at a time when Penzance was beginning to show early promise of becoming a cultural centre for the far west. He was the eldest of five children and like his younger brother John, who distinguished himself in the Army Medical Service, Humphry was bright, energetic and high spirited. He delighted in this rich rural and coastal environment, and was particularly fond of fishing. He never lost his boyhood appreciation of the countryside where science and the creative arts combine. For he was by nature a poet, and enjoyed the friendship of Coleridge, Southey, Byron, Sir Walter Scott and others. It was said that if he had not made his way in the world of science, he could equally well have done so in the artistic or literary world. He had a rare combination of talents.

Although so obviously able, he did not distinguish himself

at school, and his teacher, George Coryton, who was also a curate in Penzance, did not spare the rod and risk spoiling his lively pupil. He was wont to pull the lad's ears, and in an effort to protect himself from this painful attention young Humphry hit on the novel idea of covering them up with sticking plaster. The outgoing boy, who was popular with the other children, loved poetry and literature, and enjoyed telling stories, devising pantomimes and setting up tournaments. He became fascinated by the electrical machines and mechanical models created by a saddler called Robert Duncan, and this led to early scientific experiments making thunder powder and fireworks, resulting in quite a few loud bangs. When he was 15 he was sent to the grammar school in Truro, where Cornish worthies sent their sons in preference to public schools at a greater distance, and he now came under the tutorship of Dr Cornelius Cardew, who recognised his flair for poetry but not for science. This was surprising, for Davy was observant and had a razor-sharp, analytical mind, with the gift of seeing things in their context and recognising their potential in a much wider sphere.

Davy's father died in 1793, and two years later he was apprenticed to Dr John Bingham Borlase, a surgeon and apothecary with a flourishing practice in Penzance. This gave him the opportunity to help in the dispensary, and he also carried out experiments in the house of Dr John Tonkin, who, after a larger than usual explosion from the attic was heard to declare, 'This boy Humphry is incorrigible! He will surely blow us all up in the air some day!' Thus the lad moved in stimulating circles, and he counter-balanced his scientific activities with fishing, walking in the countryside and reading, as well as doing a little sketching and painting.

Davy's quick, lively mind made an impression on those he came in contact with, including a party of scientific men whom he escorted around the Land's End in 1797. One of their number, Dr Beddoes of Bristol was so struck with the lad, then aged 19, that he invited him to become his assistant at the Pneumatic Institution he was setting up in Bristol. This did not please Dr Tonkin who, perhaps, regarded the promising youngster as his own protegé, and wanted him to become a surgeon in Penzance. But Dr Borlase generously released him from his indentures, to take up an offer which was to lead to a brilliant career, almost unparalleled in the annals of science. Indeed, the celebrated French scientist Cuvier told the French Institute that 'Davy, not yet thirty-two, in the opinion of all who could judge of his labours, held the first rank amongst the chemists of this or any other age'.

While at Bristol Davy carried out daring experiments with laughing gas, sometimes becoming intoxicated in the process, for he saw its humanitarian application for reducing pain during surgery. This knight errant of the scientific world took considerable risks in the name of his calling, and on one occasion his promising career almost came to an untimely end through the inhaling of carburetted hydrogen. However, a recuperative spell back in the fresh air of Penzance soon drove the poison from his system, and furthermore he was to enhance his reputation by publishing his findings.

By this time he was needing more scope for his talents, and he was delighted to accept an appointment as Assistant Lecturer in Chemistry, Director of the Chemical Laboratory and, in 1801, Assistant Editor of the Journals of the newly founded Royal Institution, based at Albemarle Street in London. His salary was 100 guineas a year, with a room, coals and candles. Just over a year later he became the Royal Institution's Professor of Chemistry. Because of his interest in galvanism, he was supplied with a powerful battery of voltaic cells, which produced electricity by chemical action. This enabled him to repeat and extend experiments which he had already begun in the breaking down of compounds into their components, thereby revealing new and unsuspected elements.

Discovering that when electricity is passing through two wires, the points of the wires, when separated, are burned up by the current, he used sticks of carbon in place of the wire terminals and found that their ends leapt into radiant flame. The implications of this proved to be far reaching, for thus he gave us the electric arc lamp, the forerunner of a number of developments including the electric lamp, the Crookes tube, which gave us X-rays and radium, and also the thermionic valve, which gave us the wireless telephone. His reputation spread throughout Europe and the Institute of France awarded him the Napoleon prize of 3,000 francs for conducting the best experiments in galvanism. His achievements escalated.

In 1802 he had given a series of lectures before the Board of Agriculture on agricultural chemistry, and indeed, he came to be known as 'The Father of agricultural chemistry'. In 1803 the former lad from Cornwall achieved the rare distinction of being elected a Fellow of the Royal Society, and two years later became a Member of the Royal Irish Academy, corresponding with the most notable scientists of the day. October 19th, 1807 was a turning point in the world of chemistry, for on this day Davy first beheld the glittering globules of the new metal Potassium. This was swiftly followed by the excitement of discovering Sodium. His enthusiastic, animated style as a lecturer struck a chord with everyone, particularly the ladies, who reckoned that his attributes were cut out for other things besides 'poring over crucibles'. His poet friends declared that they went along to his lectures to learn a thing or two about the skilful use of words.

Honours abounded; in 1812 he was knighted, and also married a beautiful, wealthy widow Mrs Jane Spreece, who proved to be an asset, and a fitting partner for such a brilliant man, much in the public eye. In 1818 he was created a baronet, and two years later received the greatest accolade of his life by being elected President of the Royal Society, a position which he held for seven years. In addition to these many achievements was the founding of the Zoological Society and the invention of the miners' lamp.

After his initial departure from Cornwall in pursuit of ambition, Davy saw very little of his native county, but he retained his boyhood love of poetic and piscatorial pleasures, and made a bequest to his old school in Penzance, on the condition that the boys could enjoy an annual holiday on his birthday. But perhaps his regard for his fellow Cornishmen was best reflected in the miners' safety lamp, which won him recognition here and in places as far away as Russia. For its invention was the difference between life and death for many a miner, in the appalling conditions of the time. The fact that he never patented that invention for fear that this could restrict its use and place miners at unnecessary risk, reveals the humanitarian reasons behind a decision which could have proved highly lucrative for him.

After battling with failing health, Sir Humphry died when he was far away from home, on May 29th, 1829, and as he had requested that he be buried wherever he might die, there was a public funeral in Geneva. A tablet to his memory was also emplaced in the north transept of Westminster Abbey. The loss of one of the master spirits of the age was keenly felt. Brande, in his celebrated *History of Chemistry* described his relatively early death as 'a serious national calamity'. His centenary was celebrated by an exhibition of scientific apparatus in St John's Hall, Penzance, and a statue of him that was erected at the top of Market Street in 1872, just yards from where he was born, depicts him in his favourite coat, breeches and neck tie, holding a symbol of that famous miners' safety lamp.

Junketing at Whitsuntide

CORNISH folk worked hard and played hard. They were adept at casting work-a-day cares aside and making merry on high days and holidays, which were anticipated with great excitement and relished in retrospect. Whitsuntide, which fell at that delightful time of year in Cornwall, the beginning of Summer, invited outdoor feasting and fun.

There was a time when Whit Monday was celebrated at church houses (the vicarage or building nearby to the church) with gigantic picnics organised for the parishioners by young wardens specially appointed for this task. But by the early 19th century it became customary to wander further afield, taking picnics or calling at farmhouses to indulge in heavy cream cake, followed by junket and clotted cream. This was a rich and rare treat in their frugal lives, and junket came to be symbolic of enjoyment and extravagance; hence the term 'junketing'.

Whit Monday services were held at Gwennap Pit, a vast amphitheatre near Redruth, where John Wesley used to preach to the multitudes, and where some who came to mock were captivated by his compelling style. Gwennap Pit, which was originally a mine excavation, held a special place in the hearts of the mining fraternity, and after Wesley's death thousands of people converged here for the annual outdoor service. They came from far and wide, thronging the local highways. They came on foot, on horseback, in carriages, waggons, carts and vehicles of every description, and visiting choirs would tune up their vocal chords along the way. Vehicles crammed the vicinity, and horses were lined up along the road in the care of enterprising urchins, watchful for returning owners, and expectant of their generous tips. After the arrival of the railway, many people added the thrill of a ride in a train to their spiritually uplifting experiences at the pit.

Much of the attraction of high days and holidays stemmed from being part of a cheerful crowd, far removed from the routine. Furthermore, superstition had obligingly decreed it to be unlucky to venture afield without wearing something new. Noticing and being noticed in one's finery was part of the magic. Refreshments and a variety of attractions, seemly and otherwise took root at Gwennap Pit on these occasions, but for many, particularly the young, the religious gathering was a prelude to the more colourful delights of Redruth Fair, when the lasses eyed the lads, and the lads did their utmost to impress. The arrival of the congregation at Fair Meadow, Redruth, was heralded by the merry din of speaking trumpets, gongs, drums, organs, cymbals and excited humanity. Older folk prayed that the youngsters would remember their morals better than they themselves did in their younger days.

In 1865, the spectacular attractions of the fair included a miscellany of amazing mechanical wonders; the highly acclaimed Sanger's Waxworks, including effigies of John Wesley and the royal family, which bowed and moved speechless lips in eerie fashion and the usual Biblical scene depicting Daniel in the lion's den. There was even a mock-up of Moses in the desert, with a 'questionable fluid' running from a rock. With each passing year the travelling circuses came up with something new and exciting, and in 1877 the gaudily painted whirligigs stole the show at Redruth Fair. There was a multiplicity of agreeable diversions, particularly for young men, who had the opportunity to demonstrate their combat skills and the subtle art of self-defence by taking on antagonists who would not surrender them into the arms of the law. The popularity of

Gwennap Pit rejoicings, which left a warm glow of piety, came second only to this ancient sport of Cornish wrestling, which had a baser appeal.

All this, together with the artless fun generated by the brisk sale of 'ticklers' made for a high old time. Ticklers, which sold for a penny were little containers filled with water, used for squirting at people. And if it raised a laugh at first, amusement gave way to frustration and anger for those at the receiving end, who had had more than enough tomfoolery for one day. Folk became decidedly teasy. The shouting, swearing, scuffling and fisticuffs erupting inside the fairground, mingled somewhat incongruously with heartfelt sounds of prayer, praise and exhortation arising from an assortment of Nonconformist ministers just outside the perimeter, demonstrating perhaps, that this was truly the Lord's Day, and not exclusive to the Wesleyans or the revellers. They knew how to enjoy themselves in those days.

All For Love

IN the late 18th century, the fisherfolk of Porthgwarra lived in a world of their own, far removed from other communities by land, and unnoticed from the sea, tucked away as they were at the head of a small inlet on the western tip of Mount's Bay. Although so close to the bare and barren extremity of Land's End, the little hamlet was cosseted between the flower-strewn hills, where the humming of the bees and the sounds of the ocean blended contentedly on the summer air. But the wild Atlantic was their garden, and it governed their lives. When cruel winds howled across the western plateau and raging seas pounded relentlessly along the steep and rocky shoreline, the hardy fisherfolk of Porthgwarra hauled their boats up to a higher level, and maintained a seaward vigil until the storm abated. For these proud and handsome seafarers, said to be descendants of Spaniards cast up upon these shores, owed a debt to humanity, and were renowned for their skill and daring when it came to preserving life from the perils of the deep. One might imagine that Porthgwarra, with its background of smuggling, fishing and adventure at sea, would be remembered for its swashbuckling, colourful exploits, but strange to tell, the memory which lingers on in legend concerns the pain of true love, which never did run smoothly, and ultimate tragedy. It was a tale of a farmer's daughter and a lowly fisherman's son; a sad story of love among the crabpots.

Young Nancy was the much cherished only child of an ambitious farmer and his wife of Roskestal. They held her aloof from other children, reckoning that their daughter, with graceful manners and pleasing looks, was a cut above the rest, and destined to marry a man of substance. By contrast, young William came from hardy seafaring stock, which had never known wealth, but who were contented with their daily lives and full of warmth and love and humour. He worked as the seasons dictated, helping in the family fishing boat, sailing on small coasters, toiling on the land or turning his hand to anything that would pay. The winter when he sought employment as a serving man to the aspiring farmer up the valley served to seal his fate.

William's arrival was a day to be remembered in the lonely daughter's life, for she was captivated by this dark-eyed, handsome lad, with his cheerful quips, colourful tales and his sunny disposition. To this lonely maiden, over-protected and overwhelmed by her parents' ambitions, his arrival was like a breath of fresh air. This was the life she longed for, and his presence brought the painful, pleasurable stirrings of young love. Her heartbeat quickened as she watched him go about his daily tasks, and she winced as the master or mistress of the house exercised their sharp tongues and found fault with him. There was a transformation in her, for those wan cheeks became flushed, those sad eyes sparkled and she took to singing as she performed her daily tasks around the farm. When her parents noticed her laughing and joking with young William, they were horrified. They took her aside and scolded her for being so familiar and free with a mere serving lad. 'Have you no pride?' demanded her mother, angrily. 'What will people say when they hear that our daughter has lowered herself to speak with the servants?' This cruel reaction had the effect of making her more secretive about her daily dalliance with the fisherman's lad, for their love was truly blossoming by this time. But inevitably they were found out, and her heavy-handed father banished him from their house for ever, telling him that he was no fit suitor for their darling daughter.

True love could not so easily be torn asunder, and the young couple continued their secret assignations, in secluded lanes and quiet corners down at the fishing cove where they might be unseen. Then one day William was offered the opportunity to sail on a prolonged voyage around the world, which would take three years or so. It was his chance of wealth and riches, which might raise him in the eyes of her parents, and allow him to provide well for her as her husband. It was a heart rending decision, for they just wanted to be together, oblivious of material considerations, and it was a very sad and tearful farewell as he set sail, with both vowing to be true to each other until they were reunited.

Fair Nancy spurned the attentions of wealthy suitors who came to call, defiantly declaring that she would wed only the one she truly loved, and to whom she had plighted her troth. The fresh bloom had faded from those pretty cheeks, and she spent her days moping about the house or standing on the cliffs gazing out to sea, yearning for the return of her lover, from a spot called Hella Point which came to be known as Nancy's Garden. She grew more and more melancholy as the months rolled by. Some said the poor maid, disappointed in love, had gone out of her mind; others feared she might die of a broken heart. If her parents regretted what they had done, they consoled themselves by saying that they had her best interests at heart; who would have known that dear Nancy could have pined and suffered so?

The allotted three years came and went, without sight or sound of her beloved William. 'He's forgotten you by now, dear Nancy. Be sensible. You have many suitors; you're young and would make a good wife and mother', said her parents, now prepared to take anyone for a son-in-law, if only he could cure their lovesick daughter. 'We vowed we would meet again and marry – here or in heaven', insisted Nancy. 'And so we shall.'

One chill and moonlit winter's night when she was in her bed, she fancied that she heard him calling, 'Nancy! Nancy! Sleepest thou, Sweetheart? Awaken and come to me, my Love'. Whereupon she threw back the coverlet, rushed to the casement window and called, 'My darling William; you have come at last. Wait for me. I'm coming, I'm coming!' and ran like the wind for the cove, still dressed in her night attire. Tradition says that the sailor boy appeared to his father at about this time, telling him that he had come to claim his bride, and wishing him a final farewell.

When it was realised that the poor, demented girl had left her bed and disappeared from the house on that cold winter's night, her Aunt Prudence, who lodged at the farm rushed down to the shore in time to see the lovers sitting on a rock, spellbound in the moonlight as the tidewater rose. But as she waved and shouted to attract their attention, a sudden mist rolled in and it was said that a choir of mermaids sang in dulcet tones:

'I am thine,
Thou art mine
Beyond control.
In the wave
Be the grave
Of heart and soul.'

As the mistiness dispersed, the heads of the lovers could be seen just above the level of the water. They kissed as the waves enveloped them, and they were seen no more.

They say that poor Nancy's body was washed up a few days later, and that her lover had gone down with his ship in far away seas on that very night, and that the faithful pair were reunited in a marriage made in heaven.

The
Caradon
Adventure

THE colour and romance of brave mining endeavours have
been the inspiration for countless song writers, novelists
and movie makers the world over, but the stirring story of
Cornwall's courageous mining exploits remain virtually unsung.
Here were vision and fortitude, greed and envy and all the
human strengths and weaknesses exposed to the capricious Lady
Luck.

Caradon's successful mining adventures started somewhat
later than others around the county, making nonsense of the
old saying about there being nothing worth mining east of Truro
bridge. Although there had been small scale workings for tin
in this remote area of moorland and rough hill pasture for some
considerable time, the real wealth of these windswept uplands
remained untapped until miner James Clymo with his sons and
colleagues struck copper at South Caradon in 1837, when
copper was commanding very high prices. For the next few
decades it was to be the scene of fortunes quickly made, and
sometimes lost.

The venture took off straight away, attracting miners from
workings falling into decline in the far west of the county, paying
dividends of up to £10,000 three years later, when twelve rich

lodes extending about a mile to the north and south were being exploited, using the finest technology available at the time. Much capital was invested in the emerging mines which proliferated throughout the Caradon area. Initially the ore was transported through steep and difficult terrain by horse drawn carts to the head of the Liskeard and Looe canal at Moorswater, to be shipped from the port of Looe. But by 1846 the South Caradon and West Caradon mines were linked into the more efficient Liskeard & Caradon Railway system, which also served the Cheesewring Granite Quarry, Wheal Phoenix and other flourishing mines of the Caradon district. The railway ran a circuitous and inclined course, with a total length of eight and a quarter miles. It was customary in the early evening for the produce from the mines and quarry to be taken to Moorswater in detached trucks, which followed each other in succession, under the control of brakesmen. They were hauled back up the incline the following day by horses.

At a time when many Cornish miners were being forced to emigrate to find employment and the wherewithal to feed their starving families, this area was experiencing the heady years of success. Purpose-built townships, which still reflect the spirit of those enterprising times, mushroomed quickly, to cater for the increasing numbers of miners and their families as more and more setts were opened up. Human nature being what it is, this sudden influx of miners, who risked their lives underground in their daily toil, erupted into drunken, riotous behaviour in the streets of Liskeard of a Saturday night, after they had received their pay packets. They were a rough, tough breed of men, who worked hard and let off steam with gusto. People with social consciences made positive efforts to channel some of this excess energy into more acceptable spiritual and cultural outlets, and in March 1848 it was reported in *The West Briton:*

'The mines carried on in this neighbourhood have been the means of changing the manners and amusements of the people by introducing persons from other districts. An excellent Sunday school library, and other institutions for disseminating knowledge, have been established, and an amateur brass band has been formed, the members of which are principally miners. On Thursday the 16th instant, the band gave a ball for their friends at Tremar, in St Cleer, on the occasion of one or two of the members being about to leave this country for Australia.'

Mining is a notoriously dangerous occupation, and here, as in other mines, there were mishaps and fatalities. Cornish miners have always been very superstitious. Their philosophy was a simple, fatalistic one: 'I shall not die till my time comes'. But fearing that might come too soon, they kept anxious watch for the portents. It was deemed unlucky to see the sign of the cross on the wall of a mine, and if such a mark ever appeared, it would cause distress and be rapidly obliterated or altered. It was permissible to sing and laugh down the mines, but not to whistle or swear. The sight of a woman or a snail on the way to work augured ill; the former might tempt them to go home again, but the latter problem was more easily solved by offering the snails or 'bulhorns' some crumbs from their lunchbox or grease from their lanterns to turn bad luck to good. In cases of minor injury, miners observed the strange old custom of anointing and dressing the offending implement as carefully as the wound itself, as some sort of insurance policy of appeasement, in the hope that it would not fester. Hence the reason for neatly bandaged pickaxes and other tools of their trade sometimes seen in the mines. There was great faith in the power of divining or dowsing rods in the searching for water or mineral lodes, which has become recognised more widely. But rather less rational was the widespread belief in the little spirits or demons, said to inhabit the mines, believed to carry on the toil after mere mortals had left.

The purposeful, work-a-day scene around the mines was a noisy, industrious one, intriguing for the well-heeled sightseers who ventured this way and who were politely received. For the importance of good public relations was recognised, and their possible potential as shareholders acknowledged, particularly when fortunes were on the wane.

Boys and girls would be engaged at the buddle pits, or in jigging, screening, picking and dressing the ore. This, presumably, helped to develop the muscles, for they would gravitate into sturdy men, engaged in work between the shafts and adits, or buxom 'bal' (mine) maidens, who were employed in cobbing, breaking and assorting the ores. The bal maidens, like their male counterparts were noted for their cheeky, lively behaviour when their wearisome daily round was ended, and particularly on high days and holidays. At the centre of all this sweat and toil was the rarified, genteel world of the account house, offering decent, civilised creature comforts for the mine agents, clerks and other officials. The sightseer moving on to inspect the changing house of the working miners would have been shocked by stark, squalid conditions, and the lack of basic amenities.

In the absence of early canteens, the miners took provisions with them to sustain them through the day. Hoggans, which were hefty lumps of unleavened dough, sometimes incorporating morsels of green pork, were regarded as the traditional fare of miners. Heavy enough to demolish lesser mortals, it was a tough meal reckoned to keep a real man going all day, and more fancy fare would have invited cryptic comment from his mates at croust (lunch) time. It was a harsh, demanding way of life, even by Cornish standards and few miners lived to enjoy old age.

A miners' society was formed in East Cornwall and Devon in the mid 1860s, with the objectives of providing mutual help and co-operation among its members, charity for those in need, and solidarity, embodying the true Cornish spirit of 'one and all' when it came to the workers putting forward their requests more boldly. This was counter-productive to some extent, for after the work force of neighbouring mines went on strike, some mining managers refused to employ men from this newly formed union. But things were changing, with the spiritedness of youth, as usual. In the following decade hundreds of bal children at Caradon, working at a number of mines throughout

106

the area, went on strike for higher wages. The payment hitherto given to the girls had amounted to only six shillings a week, but those employed on the South Caradon mine bold enough to put forward their grievances and ask for more, were given an extra penny a day. When this became known in the neighbouring mine of West Caradon, the bal maidens immediately went on strike, and the agitation quickly spread to Glasgow Caradon, Marke Valley, Phoenix and other mines. At Phoenix the boys also decided to strike. In many instances the penny increase was offered, but the children demanded twopence. The managers were to witness the unprecedented sight of youngsters congregating in groups to discuss grievances and compare notes. Some of them visited the other mines to establish the general pattern of developments. Mr. West of Wheal Phoenix urged them to accept what they had been offered, and get back to work. But they refused until the demanded twopenny rise was secured. Thus remuneration for the workers was improving, but the inevitable was to happen as the mining operations ceased to be viable, in the face of foreign competition.

The glorious boom of the Caradon copper mines lasted for half a century, having experienced its ups and downs according to fluctuating world prices. Other countries like Australia, were able to exploit their mineral wealth by the process of streaming and surface mining, which was cheap to carry out in comparison with the running costs and technology required for Cornwall's deep underground mining. Some people, including a number of the finest mining captains and top personnel subscribed to the theory that if you can't beat 'em, join 'em, and left these much-loved shores to take up opportunities in every corner of the world. And indeed there was another saying to the effect that at the bottom of any big hole anywhere, you'll find a Cornish miner. Others were able to secure a satisfactory niche back home, in the developing china clay industry. But it must have been heartrending for so many Cornish families with a deep love of their homeland, to board the emigrant ships and sail away to those lands of opportunity, knowing that they would never come back. Wherever they settled, they took their culture and customs with them, refraining from work on the Sabbath and attending services in the Methodist chapels in their Sunday best in the time honoured way.

Generations on, in a vastly different social climate, the descendants of those brave, enterprising miners return to these shores to discover their Celtic roots. Those who make such pilgrimages may see distinctive features giving clues to a fascinating story of Cornish mining past; the heathery, hummocky remains of early prospecting, and a landscape dotted with humble cottages and a variety of dwellings, dominated by one, handsome house, whose owner was of some power and consequence around these parts. And of course the Wesleyan chapel, which once exercised such influence and restraint on folk's behaviour, would not be far away. A century and a half ago, industry imposed on nature; now nature has restored the *status quo*. The gigantic mounds of debris thrown up from the pits, long deserted, are now overgrown, and have become a flourishing haven for the wildlife. A suspended air of eerie quietness surrounds those handsome, ruined, ivy-grown engine houses, with their now smokeless chimney stacks reaching for heaven, remaining as proud sentinels across this former mining landscape. Those sounds of 19th century industry, the tireless hammering, the rhythmic thud of the engines, the thump, chink and clatter of horse teams, harnesses and humanity at toil have gone for ever. Long may these picturesque ruins stand as silent monuments to generations of proud endeavour and our unique Cornish heritage.

The Stranger
with Seaweed
in his Whiskers

O VER a century ago, seafarers in daily peril of the deep
believed that seagulls, with their gleaming white, ethereal
wings harboured the spirits of lost mariners, and that the cry
of a gull was that of a human soul in torture. If such a whimsical
notion be true, is it any wonder that seagulls are so plentiful
around St Ives, and their calling so plaintive and persistent?
Shipwrecks in these hazardous waters, unprotected from the
violence of the Atlantic storm, were of a particularly severe
nature and the light of many a hopeless dawn revealed the
harrowing sight of sailors and their ships cast up along these
cruel shores. And who will ever know about the numberless
vessels that disappeared without trace, leaving worried families
waiting for the loved ones who never came home? Is it any
wonder that the agonised souls of shipwrecked sailors could be
heard crying out before a brewing storm? Some said that
seafarers released from such earthly trammels eventually reach
the port of Fiddler's Green, and the calmer waters of this sailors'
heaven.

Cornish folk always regarded May as an inauspicious month,
and sailors say that whistling is unlucky, for it summons up
an ill-wind which bodes seafarers no good. So the storm one

May evening in 1862 may not have happened had some merry errand boy burst into song instead of whistling as he made his way home from a shipchandler's store. Those who had ears to hear discerned a low, uneasy chorus of suspended, seafaring spirits calling their names along the eerie, wreck-strewn shores, giving warning of a wild, south easterly storm, which was to send shipping scuttling for safe havens. The brigantine *Dove* of Devoran took a battering and the sloop *Sally* of St Ives split her jib and was driven on shore and wrecked near the breakwater.

Just after midnight Bill, a hoveller of St Ives, left his cottage and made his way to the quayside to see if any work was available in regard to the casualties of the storm. Hovellers were those who made themselves useful around the harbour, doing this and that as seafaring needs dictated, to earn a modest wage. He saw the wrecked sloop and other vessels which needed attention as he made his way along the waterfront, then just outside a tavern he noticed a figure with a crop of dark brown hair leaning against a post on the quayside. 'Good mornin' to 'ee, Stranger', he said. ''Tis a fair ol' night, to be sure. Er, do 'ee 'appen to 'ave the time?' There was no response, and feeling slightly taken aback, he moved a little closer and remarked, 'I was only bein' friendly'. There was still no response, so he added, 'Thee'rt a strange sort o' fella not to answer a cheery greetin'. Why, I'd speak to the devil 'isself, if 'ee spoke civil to me!' This drew no reply. 'Who art thou? Thou ne'd'n'st think to frighten me. If thou were'st twice as ugly thou weresn't frighten me! Who art thou?' By way of reply the stranger turned a ghastly, pallid, deathly face towards the hoveller, with larger than life eyes looming, horribly. The lifeless lips moved in the utterance of silent words, and the St Ives man noticed sand and debris clinging to the grazed face and traces of seaweed caught up in the seaman's whiskers. Then he realised the pathetic figure was sodden with seawater, and shaking and dripping in his old seaboots. He was aware of a creeping sensation in his scalp as his hair stood on end, and he shuddered, too. Not wishing to prolong the disconcerting encounter, Bill turned as coolly as he could, to walk away, but as he did so became aware of the phantom shadow at his side, matching his movements, and the muffled squelch, squelch, squelch of his companion's old seaboots. Could this be a mortal, numb with shock after experiencing disaster at sea? Should he not be helping a seafaring comrade rather than trying to escape? So he paused and turned to address the mysterious figure more kindly. The squelching stopped, but no answer was forthcoming.

The hoveller hastened along the quay to knock up one of his mates, and, glancing over his shoulder saw the eerie stranger standing where he had just left him. Bill heaved a sigh of relief, quickened his pace, and broke into a run. But his problems were not over, for the spirited stranger had arrived there before him. As he reached the front door and was about to knock, he found himself confronted by that hideous, leering face. Bill stood rooted to the spot, mesmerised, then some sort of pandemonium seemed to shake the house, as if all hell had been let loose. Time seemed to stand still while chaos reigned, and then he realised that the ghostly companion had evaporated, and all was still. Unsure what do next, he tried the door handle and stumbled inside.

It was strangely quiet in the house. 'Are 'ee there, Cap'n?' he called up the stairs in a quavering voice. 'Are 'ee awake?' This seemed a ridiculous question to ask in view of all the recent commotion. But it took several moments for his colleague to stagger out of bed to ask what he wanted. 'Strange things bin 'appening this night', said Bill, trying to regain his equanimity. ''Twas some commotion in 'ere!' he added, grasping the bannister as if emerging from a drunken stupor. 'Commotion? What do 'ee mean?' asked the surprised Captain. 'I aint 'eard nothin'. Why, what be amiss, Boy? You'm looking like wot you seen a ghost!' 'I 'ave! I 'ave. I seen a ghost!' 'Calm down, boy, and take a swig o' this 'ere. 'Ave a go at one o' my specials. Cure everything, this do, from seasickness to 'allucinations!' The frightened hoveller employed one type of spirit to banish another, and it began to take effect quite quickly. He blinked and looked around and realised that everything was intact, despite the frenzied noises he had heard.

The Captain persuaded him to carry on as usual, despite his strange experience, and they towed a stricken vessel around to Hayle. But the effects of the shock overcame him as he made his overland way home, for he collapsed senseless in the road and had to be taken the rest of the way by cart. He was tucked up in bed, where he remained for three days; all his hair fell out and he required the attention of a physician throughout the next six months.

Feat of Clay

THE discovery of china clay at Tregonning Hill by Plymouth Quaker and apothecary William Cookworthy in 1745 was a timely one indeed for the many impoverished Cornish miners. Rather than having to consider emigrating in periods of recession as others had to do before them, they had the opportunity to use their skills in this kindred new industry.

The closely guarded secret of producing finest quality pottery, known as porcelain, had originated on the Chinese mountain of Kao Lin, where the potential of the mineral which came to be known as kaolin or china clay was first exploited. The secret had reached Saxony, where a porcelain factory was established, in the 18th century. This aroused the curiosity of William Cookworthy, who managed to obtain samples for analysis, and led him to discover that it was produced from decomposing granite and feldspar, which he knew to be in the area. It was a classic case of 'eureka!' when he eventually found it.

After much exciting experimentation in his laboratory, Cookworthy took out a patent for the manufacture of porcelain in 1768, for competition was keen, and he did not want his eager rivals to benefit from the fruits of his labours. He set up a porcelain factory in Plymouth with the help of the Hon. Thomas Pitt (later to become Lord Camelford), on whose lands in St Stephen-in-Brannel he had taken out a 99 year lease. But the venture was short lived on account of technical difficulties, and the whole concern was moved to Bristol and assigned in May 1774 to Cookworthy's old friend Richard Champion.

Richard Champion, inexperienced in business and ceramics,

made attempts to extend the patent on Cornish china clay for a further 14 years, but was successfully challenged by Josiah Wedgwood, acting on behalf of other Staffordshire potters, who realised that the fine quality, whiter Cornish clays were increasingly in demand by a discerning, sophisticated market throughout the world, and sought the opportunity to exploit the situation for themselves. Wedgwood had been contravening the terms of the patent by deviously obtaining the clay through another person and having it sent on to the Midlands. This single minded businessman had upgraded the technology and perfected the high quality, inexpensive Queen's ware, much in demand, and taken positive steps to improve transportation of the raw materials to the potteries and distribution throughout Europe and beyond.

Champion, who got caught up in an astonishing maze of legal problems without deserving to do so, was no match for the determined Staffordshire potters, who were subsequently able to exploit china clay throughout the area. The needs of industry were well established in the Midlands, and it made more sense to transport the mountains of clay to their shrine, rather than attempt to establish new potteries in Cornwall where there was no coal available. This was an extremely expensive business until the purpose-built ports of Charlestown and Par on St Austell Bay made it viable. The ports enabled the precious white clay to be exported more efficiently, and opened up the worldwide markets. But by 1840 the Midland potters had relinquished their leases, and most of the pits were being operated by Cornish families, with clay being exported all over the world from Charlestown, Par, Fowey and other local ports.

Speculators around St Austell readily turned their attentions to the chalky, white treasure in the hills, which was much in demand for the manufacture of an amazing range of products worldwide, including paper, face powder and toothpaste. Banks in St Austell stayed open at all hours and did brisk business as the dusty procession of heavy clay waggons rumbled through the narrow streets, drawn by teams of horses straining at their chains and driven by straight-backed drivers, with faces and clothes whitened and stiffened with clay, resembling animated porcelain ornaments, as they cracked their whips and kept the clay trains moving.

The open cast mine at Carclaze, said to have been worked for tin since Phoenician times, was regarded as a place of beauty and wonder in the middle of the last century, when china clay was also being extracted. For the traveller it was akin to one of the wonders of the world as he suddenly came upon this enormous excavation, about a mile across and over 130 ft deep, containing streams and stamping-mills, with the strange sight of tiny figures extracting the ores far below. But the most impressive thing was the dazzling whiteness, and one visitor remarked, 'It requires, indeed, no great stretch of the imagination to fancy Carclaze a work of enchantment, and a chasm which has been opened by some potent magician in a mountain of silver'.

The secret of a Chinese mountain was transforming the Cornish landscape to such an extent that subsequent generations could scarcely imagine St Austell's hinterland looking otherwise. Just as mining settlements such as Minions and Crow's Nest had mushroomed during the tin and copper mining boom, close-knit claymining communities were established close to the pits. One such was Retew, near Indian Queens, close to Wheal Remfrey, where tin mining had been originally carried out. But its success was to be its downfall.

The area, rich in tin, iron ore and manganese, came into the possession of the Remfreys just after the Norman Conquest, and highly skilled technicians from the Harz mountains in Germany were brought here in Elizabethan times. Pearce Rogers, a Helston solicitor, took a 21 year lease on these lands in 1819, and a new pit opened up at Retew a few years later. It linked to a network of mineral railways feeding Newquay and ports on the southern coast, and was very successful.

In the good old days Retew was a happy, close-knit mining community, with the mine owner living in 'the big house'

116

employing servants, and with a specially appointed residence for the Mine Captain. There was an acknowledged hierarchy, wherein everybody recognised their place in the scheme of things. There was employment for the womenfolk, but in later years many of the wives worked in the knitting factory which was set up in the old cornmill, to manufacture interlock underwear. It was a contented, self-contained little community of the type we now look back on with great longing. Everyone knew everyone else's business (sometimes a little too well for comfort), and supported each other in times of need. They had a lively social life, organising fetes and festivals, dances and brass-band events. There was a little chapel in the village, and the children walked to school on Goss Moor. Bread, meat, groceries and the necessities of life were delivered by horse and cart, and everyone looked forward to the arrival of the friendly postman on his bike, to pass the time of day and catch up on the local news and gossip. In more affluent times they cycled to surrounding villages to attend the local 'hops', or made their way to St Dennis to sample the delights of the silver screen, and fish and chips wrapped up in newspaper, washed down with half a pint of cider, which tasted so good in the open air. Generations came and generations went, in a pattern, it seemed, which might go on for ever. Old men sat around the square, yarning with their mates in the time-honoured, Cornish style, observing, making caustic comments and remembering the good old days. Things were different in their young days, they thought, things were going downhill fast. But they did not realise quite how fast, for the claymining community had need of a guardian spirit now.

The trouble was that they were literally living on a fortune, and the powers-that-be decided that this wealth beneath their feet must be exploited; that the village of Retew should be bulldozed to make room for expansion and progress. So in the late 1960s the families gradually began to move out, and the bulldozers gradually began to move in. For a while there was an eerie period with one family after another moving out,

117

leaving the remaining community living in a ghostly village of roofless houses, faceless windows and idle doors swinging and creaking in the breeze, as cawing rooks and wildlife moved in. But even their re-colonisation was short-lived, and today all traces of the proud little mining settlement of Retew have been wiped off the face of the earth.

Christmas at
Truro Workhouse

LIFE in Cornwall was incredibly tough in former times, when ordinary folk gleaned meagre livelihoods from the sea, the land or down the mines. Yet there was a cheerful, proud and independent spirit among those hardworking people, who sometimes, through no fault of their own, fell on hard times as the result of illness, accident, unemployment or old age, and had a dread of ending up in the workhouse, dependent on charity.

Truro, which became quite a cultural and fashionable centre, with notable families living round about, had long demonstrated a concern for the poor, backed up by practical help. In the early 17th century, Jerman Griest and Henry Williams, who had both accumulated wealth in the woollen trade, had endowed almshouses in Pydar Street, together with adjacent lands for the tenants to cultivate. However, the land was taken over for the provision of a pound for stray animals, a poorhouse and a prison, neatly packaging the town's problems in one area. Public subscriptions financed a 'Publick Infirmary for the Sick, and Lame and Poor', set up in 1790 and completed nine years later, as well as a variety of humanitarian institutions, including a home for fallen women.

There were already several poorhouses in the area we now regard as Truro when a new workhouse was built at the top of St Clement's Hill in 1829, to cater for 150 people in need of help and protection. Although these institutions catered adequately for everyday needs, and were often preferable to the squalid conditions the inmates had left, it was policy not to make them too happy and comfortable, lest they might be tempted to take the easy way out, and stay on. Those who ran the workhouses were conscious of their responsibility to those who provided the charity, and those who benefited from it were made aware of their debt to society. So it was run in spartan, prison-like fashion, with inmates wearing identical uniforms, performing harsh tasks, such as the breaking up of rocks and extricating the fibre from old ropes to make oakum for caulking boats, and being subject to severe discipline, with the sexes segregated. Nevertheless, despite these daunting conditions, this hated workhouse, like many others, remained filled to capacity.

But Yuletide was the time to relax the austerity and attempt to provide a little Christian warmth and good cheer, as demonstrated by this letter of 1867 describing Christmas Day in the Truro workhouse:

'Sir. It is gratifying to know that while every family that could afford it were enjoying the good things with which Christmas is celebrated, the large and unfortunate family, consisting of the aged and infirm, the destitute and helpless, now in our workhouse, were not forgotten. On Christmas day, the inmates, to the number of 255, were supplied with a dinner of roast beef and plum pudding, and after they had partaken of these to their full content, the old men were treated with what to many of them was a real luxury, pipes and tobacco, the old women with snuff with which to tickle their olfactory nerves; and the children with oranges and nuts. In the evening they were all provided with a bountiful supply of excellent cake and tea. It is scarcely necessary to say that the whole was greatly enjoyed. The dining hall had been most profusely and tastefully festooned and decorated with evergreens and artificial flowers, interspersed with Chinese variegated lamps, by the superintendent of labour and the porter, and its appearance in the evening when lighted by the coloured lamps, was strikingly brilliant and pleasing.'

120

A hundred and twenty years later, my colourful old friend John Cockle, seafarer, raconteur, the somewhat larger-than-life son of a Ghanaian sailor who ran away to sea, and a particularly prim and upright, God fearing English mother, was sitting by the blazing Yuletide log, reminiscing about Christmases past in Truro. 'We had good times', he mused, his eyes twinkling with pleasurable nostalgia. 'We had happy times here, in Truro. It has always been a metropolitan kind of a place with the influx of seafarers and such, providing a lively mix, and we Truronians have always known how to celebrate. Well known for it!' He looked thoughtful for a moment, then anticipating the opportunity to exploit a promising situation to good effect, added gravely, 'But I'd like to tell you about the Christmas I spent in the workhouse! Whether they were the 'Good Old Days' for everybody is an interesting point. Yes, I recall this particular Christmas very clearly indeed; I was about five or six at the time . . . '

His mother was a staunch member of the Salvation Army in Truro. The Band of Hope had a great following in those days and it was customary for members of the 'Sally Army' to give concerts at the workhouse as a Christmas treat for the inmates. It was in the nature of a charitable act, and they would be entertained with songs, music, recitations and suchlike. His mother used to play the mandolin and sing, and he and his three brothers were expected to sing with her. For weeks she had been teaching them the carol *Once in Royal David's City,* and another piece called *Summerland.*

Having been scrupulously scrubbed, decked out in their Sunday best and reminded about good manners, the family duly set out for the workhouse, with Mrs Cockle wheeling the two smaller boys in the pushchair, while young John trotted alongside carrying the mandolin. As they went along, they met up with other Salvationists, conspicuously carrying their instruments to the concert.

Arriving at the workhouse, they were ushered into a large hall, suitably decorated for the festive season, but nevertheless, somewhat overpowering in its austerity. The room was crowded with people, but they were subdued, and the atmosphere was tense. The inmates were carefully positioned in readiness for the entertainment, with boys wearing dark suits and hob-nailed boots seated on the floor at one side, and girls in thick skirts and pinafores on the other. Behind them were the men in thick, dark suits occupying rows of wooden forms, respectably segregated from the women dressed in identical bonnets and shawls. In addition to this were the 'tramps' as they were referred to, easily distinguishable from the rest, who happened to be passing through at the time, and thus retained a certain individuality.

The concert began, and nervous singing and music filled the air; but the atmosphere remained tense as shy inmates stared at embarrassed performers. Smatterings of applause at a given signal greeted the end of each well-rehearsed performance, and then it was the turn of the Cockle family, who sang their hearts out in an attempt to please. As luck would have it, the end of their contribution coincided with the interval, and the sounds of scuffling feet mingled with weak applause as most of the inmates shuffled out, leaving those with stronger bladders sitting impassively gazing at the entertainers, as they sat awkwardly attempting to demolish caraway seed buns politely, and sipping weak, sickly-sweet tea from hefty mugs. Mrs Cockle, who kept an anxious, firm watch on her brood, made it plain that they must finish up their refreshments and empty their mugs to show that they appreciated the kindness and hospitality. John chuckled at the recollection, 'I managed to get through that awful bun, but have never touched seedycake to this very day!'

Daylight was fading and the gas lamps were being lit in the streets outside as the captive audience took its place for the second part of the concert. The closing number was greeted with enthusiastic applause, but whether this signified appreciation, or relief that the concert was at an end was unclear and after suitable words of charitable sentiment were exchanged the inmates clattered their way back to their quarters. The

Salvationists thankfully gathered up their instruments and emerged into the cold streets of Truro to wend their way home, revelling in the fresh air and freedom on that moonlit Boxing Day night.

Moonshine
in Polperro

SMUGGLING was rife around the coast of Cornwall, but it was the quaint and charming little port of Polperro which achieved the dubious distinction of having Britain's first Preventive Service unit. Polperro, with its engaging hotchpotch of fishermen's cottages clinging to the hillside, narrow streets, secret passages and a profusion of hiding places was perfect for the pursuit of smuggling, with easy access to the water and up the valley to aid swift operations. The whole set-up in Polperro and the neighbouring countryside was slickly organised, for when the call came, the smith left his forge, the baker his oven and the farmer his plough. The women worked hand in glove with their husbands and sweethearts, and the children, who knew all about keeping 'mum', also had a role to play. Horrifying tales of ghosts and hauntings around Polperro and Talland played a useful part in keeping inquisitive mortals at bay. Successful runs across the water brought consignments of wines, spirits, tobacco, silk, lace, perfume and other luxuries to satisfy the gentry, magistrates, the parson, the inn keeper and others with the money to pay. Contraband goods were hidden locally before being taken along the line for distribution, but sometimes it was prudent to hide them on weighted rafts, to be collected when the coast was clear.

In the heyday of smuggling at Polperro, the activities were largely influenced by an enterprising rascal called Zephaniah

Job, known to one and all as the 'Smugglers' Banker'. This St Agnes man, who became a mine captain, had been obliged to leave his home area with indecent haste after being involved in a violent brawl. But, nothing daunted, he came here and, of all things, set up his own school, of questionable benefit to the fisherfolk's children. He was a personable rogue. One thing led to another, and he acquired the harbour rights, a fleet of fishing vessels and acted as an accountant, solicitor and general business adviser, setting up his own bank and producing his own currency. He was clever enough to direct operations without getting implicated, and made a fortune out of privateering. He lived like a lord, but also performed some good works, such as the improvement in coastal communications, and left a large bequest to his administrators.

After the arrival of the unwelcome Preventive men in the smugglers' midst, it was an on-going battle of wits. The wise smuggler was wont to remove the evidence as quickly as possible, for the Preventive boats were continually snooping around these waters, 'creeping' – dragging the sea bed with grapnels to locate the rafts with hidden consignments, which brought them prize money. The penalties for being caught out were severe. Was the 'Moonshine Brigade' motivated entirely by the acquisition of money? Or was it the excitement and adventure that made smuggling so compelling?

Smuggling stories still have the power to enthrall, and fishermen have always been known to spin a good yarn, particularly in the tavern, where it helped to keep their tankards topped up. A tale told by Young Jimmy, in the early 1900s concerned his father, who survived many a seafaring skirmish and close squeak during his colourful smuggling career, which he regarded as an honourable calling. It seems that Old Jimmy, who had sought to be prudent with his ill-gotten gains had concealed £500 in the massive chimney of his cottage. This seemed to be highly fortuitous on the face of it, but there was a small technicality which would prevent him from enjoying these fruits of his endeavours. The money, made up of single pound notes was issued by Zephaniah Job's bank, and the bank had just failed. Something needed to be done – and done quickly.

For years Old Jimmy and his confederates had made runs across to Brittany under cover of darkness, always exchanging their currency for consignments of top quality brandy. No one on this side of the Channel was likely to accept the bank notes, but if they were quick, there might be a chance to do one last deal with the Bretons before the news filtered through. Old Jimmy was well past his seafaring days, so it fell to Young Jimmy and his grandson Jimmy's Jimmy to carry out the audacious plan.

The two hastily set about obliterating distinguishing features on the old family lugger, altering the nameboard, registration port and changing to sails of a different colour, before setting off, hopefully for the coast of Brittany, in a rising gale. The god of storms was the smugglers' divinity, for foul weather tended to keep the Preventive men in port, and allowed the smuggler to sharpen his skill and mastery against the elements. So they prayed for a deterioration in the weather, and a successful mission.

If the two men had any misgivings about their dubious dealings across the Channel, they looked the bartering Frenchman straight in the eye, shook hands on the deal with great cordiality and beat a hasty retreat, not daring to look back. Then it was up with the sails and off, into the very teeth of a now ferocious gale, beneath a menacing midnight sky. Their prayers had been answered thus far, but the return trip proved to be quite a bounce for even these hardened seafarers. However, they had a certain consolation in seeing the King's cutters taking refuge from the storm, and veered down Channel to deposit their goods on a specially constructed raft in a sheltered bay. The raft was weighted and sunk, to be retrieved another day.

As it transpired, the whole operation went like a charm. The goods were safely landed and conveyed to Bodmin Moor, where scores of ankers of brandy were regularly stored, before reaching their established outlets. 'The ol' Preventive men didn't prevent we!' chuckled Young Jimmy. 'So we more than doubled our money in the space of one week!' And his bright eyes would twinkle merrily beneath his bushy eyebrows at the satisfying recollection.